Mapping Your Volunteer Vacation

Jane Stanfield

Where Is She Heading

Where Is She Heading

This workbook is designed to provide information about the subject matter covered. It is sold with the understanding that the publisher and the author are not engaged in rendering legal, accounting, or other professional services. If expert assistance is required, the services of a competent professional should be sought.

It is not the purpose of this workbook to reprint all the information that is otherwise available to travelers and volunteers but to complement, amplify, and supplement other texts. For more information, see your bookstore.

Every effort has been made to make this book as complete and accurate as possible. However, there may be mistakes both typographical and in content. Therefore, this text should be used only as a general guide and not as the ultimate source of volunteer vacationing or traveling. Furthermore, this book contains information on volunteer agencies and travel information that is current only up to its printing date.

The purpose of this workbook is to educate and entertain. The author and Where Is She Heading shall have neither liability nor responsibility to any person or entity with respect to any loss or damage caused or alleged to be caused directly or indirectly by the information contained in this workbook.

If you do not wish to be bound by the above, you may return this book to the author for a full refund. If you find any mistakes, please send your corrections to the author for the next edition.

Permissions

Packing list from Changes in Latitude, Boulder, CO **www.cil.com**

Time Zone Map from Wikimedia 2007 CIA World Facebook

Books may be ordered in quantity and/or special sales by contacting the publisher Where Is She Heading, P.O. Box 27482, Lakewood, CO 80227, 303-988-1356, email at **mappingyvv@me.com** or with the order form in the back of the book.

Published by: Where Is She Heading, **www.whereissheheading.com**
10879 W. Dartmouth Ave., Lakewood, CO 80227 U.S.A.

Book cover design and interior layout by Ronda Taylor, Taylor by Design (**www.taylorbydesign.com**)

Library of Congress Control Number 2008909439

ISBN 978-0-9821282-0-6

First Edition   Printed in Canada

ENVIRONMENTAL BENEFITS STATEMENT

Where is She Heading saved the following resources by printing the pages of this book on chlorine free paper made with 100% post-consumer waste.

TREES	WATER	ENERGY	SOLID WASTE	GREENHOUSE GASES
7 FULLY GROWN	2,538 GALLONS	5 MILLION BTUs	326 POUNDS	611 POUNDS

Calculations based on research by Environmental Defense and the Paper Task Force. Manufactured at Friesens Corporation

Acknowledgments

I am deeply indebted to the many wonderful people in my life and in the publishing industry mentioned below. In several cases, I have included websites or email addresses for more information.

The trip that inspired this book would never have happened without the following people: James C. and Marjorie Stanfield, my parents; Anne Stanfield-Hagert, sister and baboon-inspired impetus to go international; Peter J. Hughes, mentor, friend, teacher of Your Heart's Desire at MRS in Denver, and believing eyes for everything I endeavor (www.peterjhughes.com); Shane Delavan, financial healer; Karen Stickland, my main "go-to" person while I was away; and Brett and Betty Schmitt, pet wranglers extraordinaire.

Thanks to the following people who stood behind me and supported me in glorious and powerful ways both in the planning stages and when I was traveling abroad: Dr. Kris Abbey (www.hampdenfph.com), Diane Ahonen, Kerry Beebe, Ray, Angela and Sophie Berry, Lana Calhoun, Bob Delavan, Dan Dilley (www.dilleyprinting.com), Laura DiMinno (www.spiritinsession.com), Noreen Doyle, Bette Flagler, Bonnie and Susan Hickey, Faythe Houston, LaDonna Jurgensen, Sharon Kirby-Cole, Dr. Ryan Kramer, Cyndi Mancinelli, David Maurek, Patrick McAfee, Terri O'Hara (www.animalwize.com), Annemarie Potter, Arlene Rapal, Bill and Sherry Scebbi, Mary Schroeer, Janis Stephenson, Sharon Tave, Candy Vande Ven, Tamera Vander Vliet, Robbie Weadick, Meredith Williams, Carole Wood (www.mkicountry.com).

To these preliminary readers and fellow volunteers, I am deeply grateful: Sue Asher, Robert Brody, Laura DiMinno, Elizabeth Enas, Thornton and Anne Hagert, Bonnie and Susan Hickey, Sally Kurtzman, Jennifer Lauer, Tom Michelson (www.airtreks.com), Shawn Nawrocki, Roger Prior, Suzanne Stone, Judith Strobel, and Karen Van Cleve.

Finally, this book would never have come to fruition without the following people: Faye Quam Heimerl (www.quameditorial.com) the content editing, Barbara McNichol (www.barbaramcnichol.com) the line editing and proofreading, Joyce Miller (www.writerservices.biz) the quotation permissions, Ronda Taylor (www.taylorbydesign.com) layout and cover design, and Cameron Fay at Fiesens for printing (www.friesens.com).

Contents

Part One: 12 to 6 Months Before You Leave

Part Two: 8 to 6 Months Before You Leave

Part Three: 3 Months to 1 Month Before You Leave

Part Four: 1 Month to 1 Week Before You Leave

Part Five: It is Time to Go!

Part Six: Special Trips

Part Seven: Resources

How To Use This Book

Welcome—and thank you for accepting my invitation to consider a volunteer vacation. As a volunteer, you will be giving your time and talents and receiving exploration and learning. *Mapping Your Volunteer Vacation* helps you investigate ahead of time everything you'll need to know, plan, do, prepare for, and pack to embark upon and enjoy your adventure.

I have been where you stand now, as I took a year to plan a yearlong trip to volunteer my way around the world. Thankfully, I am a planner at heart. It is part of my joy. I had not found a single source that laid out the steps I needed to complete before I left. So I created this book for myself and for others like me.

I wrote this book with an individual or a couple in mind, as opposed to a group. It is geared for a single volunteer vacation found through a placement agency and lasting fewer than four weeks. By skimming the entire book before you begin, you will see the organization and progression involved. Then, based on your trip's preparation timeline, you will know when to delve into each chapter.

If you're exploring the idea of a volunteer vacation or international travel for the first time, I invite you to take your time. PART ONE of the book will lead you through the questions WHY, WHAT, WHERE, WHO, WHEN, and HOW MUCH. It will not give you specific answers, as those will be personal to you. Rather, it will provide ideas and topics to think about, help you clarify your goals, and assist in selecting the right volunteer experience for you.

PART TWO will guide you through health and passport issues, air reservations, plans for what you will do on your vacation, and logistics to keep order at home while you are away. PART THREE presents issues to consider such as lodgings and cultural research while you are on your trip, and PART FOUR provides suggestions on practical issues such as packing, money, and how to prepare in advance to return home. PART FIVE helps you with all the details to get you ready to be away. PART SIX discusses planning for longer trips, group or family travel, and what to consider when looking for volunteer work without the help of an agency.

PART SEVEN is a resource section in which I list sources of further information on both volunteer vacations and general travel. The list will give you a good start but does not cover every possible resource.

Many of you may already be savvy volunteers and international travelers. For you, this book can act as a checklist for what you already know and provide reminders that can make your next volunteer vacation unique from all your previous vacations.

Each chapter and topic offers suggestions only. Any manner of preparation that works for you is valid. I am offering the progression I used to prepare for my own trip. I encourage you to use what fits for you and your trip and leave the rest.

Throughout the chapters, you will find icons presenting additional information. Here is a "map" legend of the icons:

Map pin – Hints or tips about the topic discussed

Compass – Items that will be specific to your trip and may require research

Suitcase – Personal stories from my trip around the world

As you know, some data can only be guaranteed accurate up to the date of printing. Any prices quoted in this book are in U.S. dollars, unless otherwise specified. Please remember they are meant as general guidelines.

I am extremely excited for you as you start your journey. After you have returned, I welcome your comments on your experience with this book and your volunteer vacation. Feel free to send your input either via email at **mappingyvv@me.com** or use the postcard at the back of the book.

I leave you to plan your dream with one of my favorite quotations about being a volunteer:

> *"Volunteers don't get paid, not because they are worthless, but because they are priceless."* — **Sherry Anderson**

I wish for you a wonderful journey, and a safe return. Happy mapping.

Jane Stanfield

There are several charts and forms in this workbook. If you prefer to fill them out on your computer, go to **www. janestanfieldwish.com** and find the link for MYVV Forms. To access the forms, the password is VOLUNTEER.

A Word from the Author

I offer this book as a guide to ease your way for planning a volunteer vacation. The year I spent planning my volunteer vacation would have been much easier using a resource like this.

I sincerely hope this book helps you address all the questions you face before you lock the door, head for the airport, and travel the world.

Take your dream and make it a reality by following this map. Get out there and SHINE!

Hold the World in Your Heart . . . Volunteer.

Jane Stanfield
January 2009

"I have wandered all my life, and I have also traveled; the difference between the two being this, that we wander for distraction, but we travel for fulfillment." — **Hilaire Belloc**

Part One: 12 to 6 Months Before You Leave

After Part One, you will have:

- ❏ Skimmed Mapping Your Volunteer Vacation
- ❏ Read Chapters 1 to 6
- ❏ Begun to determine:
  - ❏ Why you want to volunteer
  - ❏ What you want to do as a volunteer
  - ❏ Where you want to go
  - ❏ Whom you want to work with and for
  - ❏ When you can go and for how long
- ❏ Gotten a feel for volunteer placement fees and what they include
- ❏ Developed a tentative schedule and alerted the appropriate people

1 Why...

Right from the outset, I think it is important to establish the basis for your journey. What is a *volunteer?* The word is a noun, commonly defined as somebody who works without being paid. What is a *vacation?* Another noun, this word is almost universally understood as time devoted to rest, travel, or recreation. When combined, these two words might be called a vacation with heart, a trip that makes a difference, or traveling with the purpose to do good in the world.

Volunteer vacationing is growing in popularity as proven by the burgeoning number of agencies that offer this type of trip, both in the United States and abroad. More and more people are doing it. Why?

Why Volunteer While on Vacation?

Why would anyone take a *volunteer* vacation when they could take a regular relaxing vacation? In my experience, people volunteer because they:

- Get to explore new places

- Meet new people

- Are eager to try something new

- Want to make a difference

- Learn about themselves

- Stretch their capabilities

- Like to act as unpaid ambassadors for their country

- Want to see what it feels like to live abroad

- Feel good about themselves afterward

- May be eligible for a tax deduction on their travel and vacation

- Find volunteering fun

An Opportunity to Learn

When I volunteer, I always look forward to learning something new. During my year abroad, the volunteer experience least like my daily life was the archaeological dig with Earthwatch in Thailand. I had ignored my father's advice when he counseled me to study subjects in college such as archaeology, languages, and philosophy. During my volunteer work at the dig, I was able to go back to "college," ask questions, and study with the best of the best.

Earthwatch places volunteers with renowned scientists, and I worked side by side with graduate students, and international and local professionals. Every night after dinner, I attended presentations on the data I was helping to collect. The best part about this "college experience" was I did not have to take notes, write exams, or worry about grades! In fact, I enjoyed it so much, I went back the next year for the final dig for the primary investigator at the site.

Why Do You Want to Volunteer?

The most satisfied volunteers are clear about their motivation for volunteering and plan their vacations accordingly. Please rank in order of importance why you want to volunteer.

When I volunteer, I want to:	Rank
Try something new	
See new places	
Meet new people	
Use my current skills	
Learn a new skill	
Learn a new language	
Meet a potential partner	
Share my knowledge and skills with others who can't afford to pay	
Serve others in need	
Other (see previous list):	

When you open the Charting Your Course foldout in the back of the book, you can begin to explore possible routes for your volunteer vacation. You may want to keep this foldout open as you work through the book—especially for Part One.

Why Pay to Volunteer?

Volunteer vacations are meant to be a win-win-win situation for the non-governmental agencies (NGOs) in the country(ies) in which you volunteer, the volunteer placement agencies, and you.

To reach their goals, most NGOs need financial as well as work contributions from volunteers. The fees paid to the volunteer placement agency you select cover expenses such as pre-trip paperwork, project literature and volunteer handbooks, training, housing and meals, insurance, and occasionally, partial financing of the in-country projects.

To help them locate willing and qualified volunteers, foreign NGOs often partner with Western nonprofit or for-profit placement agencies. You may find these advantages of using a placement agency to be significant:

- The agency provides you with one-stop shopping for information on what to expect, where you will stay, and the work you will do as a volunteer.

- Many agencies offer established, ongoing volunteer projects with a proven track record.

- You experience predictability and consistency of what you do from day to day at your volunteer worksite.

- You see firsthand what your money supports. For example, it may pay for local workers to help when no volunteers are available; supplies for schools, libraries, and clinics; food and clothing for orphans or other children; food and supplies for wildlife programs, etc.

The Win-Win-Win Benefits of Volunteering

In-Country NGO Receives...	Placement Agency Receives...	You Receive...
Much-needed funding for projects	People to help the NGOs	Deeper and richer travel experiences
Extra hands for the work	People who will act as unpaid ambassadors for the their country	Greater understanding of cultures different from your own
Your expertise and special skills	People with the time and financial resources to go volunteer	A chance to serve
Your openness to experience something new, your flexibility, and your sense of adventure	Financial resources for marketing, locating, and preparing additional volunteers	A possible tax deduction

The bottom line is you are paying to volunteer not only to support and enhance the lives of others but to hopefully enrich your own life. In return for your service, you can experience an extraordinary vacation with heart!

Volunteering Vacations = Tax Deductions?

If you are placed through a recognized, U.S., 501(c)(3) volunteer agency, a portion of your fee paid to the agency may be tax deductible. For example, the portion of the fee that is used to house and feed a volunteer plus the amount that is an outright donation to the NGO is generally tax deductible. At the end of the fiscal year, you should receive a letter from the nonprofit with the dollar amount of your fee that may be tax deductible. According to the IRS, in order for the cost of your volunteer work to be tax deductible, you must work at least eight hours a day as a volunteer. If the majority of your trip is for volunteer work, other out-of-pocket expenses, such as transportation, vaccinations, lodgings and visas, may also be tax deductible. Keep receipts for your accountant or tax advisor. The IRS website has several bulletins about charitable gifts and donations. Check out **www.irs.gov/formspubs/index.html**.

As you can see, people leave home to volunteer either within the U.S. or abroad for many reasons. What reasons appeal to you? Do you seek connections? Would you like the adventure of experiencing a new culture, language, or landscape? Or do you perhaps long to escape from your routine and try something totally different? Whatever your reason, an agency, organization, or cause is looking for you.

Once you know *why* you want to volunteer, your next mapping decisions are *what*, *where*, *who*, and *when*.

Notes

2 What...

What can you do as a volunteer? Almost anything. If you already know exactly what you want to do, great! If not, that's okay. This book is here to help you explore possibilities.

What Work Is Available?

By doing a little research beforehand, you can decide if a particular type of work is a good match for your volunteer vacation goals. Pull out the **Charting Your Course** foldout in the back of the book and the grid that follows. You may be surprised at the diversity of volunteer opportunities available. To help you narrow down the type of work you want to do, you might look through the following options and circle your preferences.

What Are Your Work Preferences?

Scope and type of work	Inside	Outside
	Easy	Strenuous
	Independent	With a team
	Unskilled labor	Skilled labor
Physical requirements	Hiking	Lifting
	Carrying – short distance	Carrying – long distance (or # of miles or hours a day)
	Physical labor	Sedentary
Language	English required	English preferred
	Ability to speak the local language, beginning level	Fluent in local language
Expertise (TEFL = Teaching English as a Foreign Language)	Required certification (e.g. TEFL, SCUBA)	Desired certification (e.g. TEFL, SCUBA)
	Required degrees: MD, RN, JD	Preferred degrees: MD, RN, JD
Demographics of people you wish to assist	Newborns/Infants	Toddlers
	Children	Teens
	Adults	Elderly
	Special needs (ADD, ADHD, etc.)	Disabled
	Same race	Different race
	Same religion	Different religion
Wish to work with . . .	People	Data
	Animals or plants	Inanimate objects
Skill preference	Use an existing skill	Learn a new skill

An Excellent Resource

Want to get a feel for agencies offering volunteer work that fits your interests and parameters? Check out **www.idealist.org**. This website allows you to sort not only by type of work, but also by length of stay, country, time of year, range of dates, and cost.

Age Limits and Local Language

Age - Every volunteer placement agency can provide you with the age requirements for its various volunteer opportunities. The range is generally between 17 and 80. Children under 17 may be accepted, when accompanied by a parent or legal guardian. I have worked on 14 different teams with volunteers ranging from 17 to 75 years of age. Everyone was able to help in some way, regardless of age or physical ability.

Language - In most cases, you do not have to know the local language at your work site. Someone usually speaks English. However, if you want to communicate in the local tongue, ask if local language lessons will be offered. If not, find out if an interpreter will be present. I have been placed by six different agencies on five continents, and English was spoken on all of the work sites. However, I found it beneficial to have some command of the local languages when in town or on the way to my sites.

Now that you have narrowed down the type of work you prefer as a volunteer, please list and rank the work specifics that best suit you.

Type and Scope of Volunteering I Want to Do	Rank

Volunteer Bob, a fellow volunteer working with orphans in Peru through Global Volunteer, asserts, "Don't be intimidated if you don't know the language. Amazing amounts of communication can happen with sign language, a smile, and pictures."

If you are where I was at this point in the process, everything sounds fun and exciting. If you do not have a solid idea of what you want to do, the next four questions should help you find some answers.

Even though you may focus on one or two options on the following pages as you continue, I encourage you to keep a running list of other interests for the future. By now you know you have a world of choices!

Notes

Notes

3 Where...

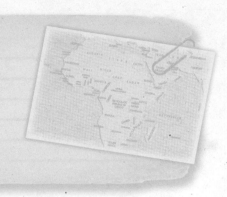

Where do you want to volunteer? The world is a big place with limitless possibilities, and your head may be spinning as you try to pinpoint the perfect trip. You might start by considering countries where you have enjoyed taking regular vacations.

Even with that, you may have more choices than time. Perhaps continue your wish list of different volunteer vacations based on both the What and Where chapters.

Your Travel Goals

This chart should help you think about your travel goals based on a location. Please rank these goals in order of importance.

When I Travel I Want To...	Rank
Revisit a favorite country	
Explore a new country	
Visit a place I have read about	
Discover my ancestral homeland	

If you have already decided your destination(s), you are on your way. If not, the table on the next page may help you focus your options. Circle the conditions of greatest interest to you.

Seasons

As you plan the timing of your trip, consider if you would like to see or work with something that happens only once a year (e.g., migration of a favorite animal, specific flowers or crops in bloom, etc.).

Migration

Migration can mean more than just animals. Don't forget the regular tourist season. Do you want to mingle mostly with the locals or with other out-of-towners, too? Consider not only standard U.S. vacation periods, but also vacation times for other nations, as well as traditional holidays in your target country.

Optimal Location Conditions (for You)

Climate	Tropics	Temperate
	Desert	Arctic
Weather/Season What clothing do you like to wear?	Spring	Summer
	Autumn	Winter
Altitude	Sea level	Mountainous
Hemisphere (Remember, the seasons are reversed!)	Northern	Southern
Time Zones	North America	Europe
	Within 6 zones	Other side of the world (12 zones away)

Distance

If you are able to volunteer for only a short time (two weeks or less), are you willing to take long flights and deal with possible jetlag? Can you find a similar opportunity closer to home, or at least in your time zone? (If you are from the United States, you might consider Mexico, Canada, Central America, South America, or the Caribbean.)

Notes

Consulates

I had already planned to go to Peru to volunteer, and Machu Picchu was on my list of sightseeing destinations while on vacation. At a Denver book signing with travel writer Elliot Hester, author of *Adventures of a Continental Drifter*, I encountered a woman who turned out to be the Consul from the Peruvian Consulate in *Denver*. I was shocked! I thought all embassies and consulates were on either one of the coasts in cities such as Washington DC, New York, or Los Angeles. I discovered that not only did the Denver area have a Peruvian Consulate, but also it has 10 other consuls and consulates.

I decided to take advantage of this discovery and visited the Peruvian Consulate in Denver. I came away with a wealth of information that opened my eyes to the amazing variety of activities and sights to see while in Peru. (For a description of the differences between an Embassy and a Consulate, please refer to Chapter 28: Glossary.)

Where Will You Be Comfortable?

You are more apt to enjoy your volunteer vacation and be enthusiastic about the project if you are physically comfortable. Knowing your preferences for accommodations, food, and recreation will allow you to choose a volunteer program that fits your needs and style.

Luxury?

Keep in mind it is *highly unlikely* you would find luxury hotel accommodations when working on a wildlife placement in the bush of a developing country.

Roommate

Note: It is common for a standard accommodation to include one or more same-sex roommates. If you prefer your own room, you will probably pay an additional fee.

Lodging, catering, restroom, and bathing arrangements can run the gamut from quite comfortable and familiar with western plumbing to charmingly rustic with a travel trailer and portable toilets or really roughing it with tents and holes in the ground. Accommodations depend mainly on the type of volunteer work you select. The volunteer agency literature should give you an accurate picture of the type of food offered, standard toilet and bathing facilities, housing and roommate arrangements.

Your Preferences

To help you define your needs and style, circle your range of preferences:

Accommodations – hotel, guesthouse, home stay, bunkhouse, or tent

Room occupancy – single, couple, roommates, or family

Roommates – none, one, two, three or more, same-sex, or coed

Toilets – Western plumbing, European plumbing (bidet), squat toilets, trench toilets, or bush

Bathing facilities – communal showers, sun showers, or private bath (en-suite)

Dining – restaurants, local cooks, communal cooking, or self-catering (Self-catering can range from you cooking food that is supplied to buying and cooking your own food.)

Site location – urban, suburban, rural, bush, or whoop whoop (Australian for as far out and remote as you can get!)

Proximity to phones/Internet – on-site, walking distance, local village, or the next city

Proximity to recreation – on-site, walking distance, or travel by bus or car

Proximity to Recreation

Depending on the type of placement and location, after-work recreation may range from scarce to a party every night.

While working with orphans in Peru through Global Volunteers, the volunteers were housed in a small hotel, and our group walked to different restaurants every night. Conversely, while working at wildlife rehabilitation centers in Australia and South Africa, we were miles from the closest town and usually in an area without TV reception. Our evening activities involved watching fantastic sunsets, listening to animal sounds as they bedded down, and reading from the considerable lending library left by previous volunteers.

Both types of recreation can be fun. Which do you prefer?

As you explore options, you may discover parameters with higher priorities that will help you select your agency and volunteer vacation choice.

Notes

4 Who...

At the volunteer site, you will be working in a community of other volunteers as well as local workers, which presents a great opportunity to develop friendships. The people who help you arrange your vacation and those you work with once you've arrived can make a major difference in your enjoyment of the whole experience.

With whom would you like to work? This section addresses both the volunteer placement agency and your fellow volunteers.

Volunteer Organizations or Agencies

If you're already familiar with an organization or agency you wish to work with or for, you have a great start. If not, there are different types of agencies to consider. Some of the factors involved might make a difference and influence your decision. Researching agencies to find a good fit before you pay your deposit is recommended. Consider:

U.S. nonprofits – If you work for a U.S. nonprofit, a portion, and sometimes a sizeable portion, of your placement fee will probably be tax deductible. While not always an accurate indicator, an organization with a website address ending in "dot-org" is usually classified as a U.S. nonprofit by the IRS.

U.S. for-profit volunteer agencies – A growing number of U.S. for-profit companies offer volunteer vacation opportunities. These website addresses usually end in "dot-com". Be sure to ask the agency which of your trip expenses may be eligible for tax deductions and consult your tax advisor as well.

 Be Aware

Not all U.S. nonprofits can provide you with legitimate tax deductions. For example, if the primary mission of an agency is lobbying, donations may not be tax deductible according to the IRS. It's best to confirm with the volunteer placement agency the tax deductibility of fees for your specific volunteer vacation.

Foreign nonprofits – I found the expenses working through these agencies to be generally less costly per week than U.S. nonprofits, but I did not receive a U.S. tax deduction for their fees. Other expenses however, such as airfare, visa, vaccinations, lodgings, and local transportation, may be deductible.

Agency mission statement and/or affiliations – Reading the agency brochures and pre-trip literature should help you determine if the agency is a good fit for you. Does it require you to belong to its organization or act as its ambassador while you work? Do you agree with the principles outlined in its mission statement?

Date founded – Volunteer vacations have been offered for some time, but recently the number of agencies offering this kind of trip have dramatically increased. To assure the agency fits your goals, read their literature thoroughly. See if it states the founders and date begun, lists the board of directors and major donors, and describes where and how the agency allocates its money.

Local Information Events

Some of the larger agencies (for example, Peace Corps or Earthwatch) offer informational events, or fairs, several times a year. Contact your local branch or the main office for information on upcoming events in your area. These events provide excellent opportunities to ask previous volunteers about their experiences. You may even find someone with direct experience or knowledge about the *exact site* you are considering. It can be a fun evening of research for you.

Who Else Volunteers?

With whom would you like to work at your volunteer site? This is good to know, as some volunteer agencies attract specific ages, genders, and nationalities. For example, I found foreign-managed agencies and U.S. agencies with offices in several countries drew volunteers from many nations. Agencies that offer a wide range of volunteer activities, and especially those requiring lots of physical activity, usually appeal to a young, athletic demographic.

While the characteristics of your volunteer team can never be 100 percent guaranteed in advance, you should be able to find agencies that attract the type of co-workers you prefer by carefully reading agency literature and asking questions of the staff and previous volunteers.

Lifelong Friends

As I left for my year around the world, my first two goals were to volunteer and vacation. Being a single woman in my 40s, my third goal, in the back of my mind, was to meet a handsome gentleman. However, the majority of my co-volunteers turned out to be women, a situation similar to my volunteer experiences in the U.S. The most common ratio of women to men that I encountered as an international volunteer was 70:30.

Some agencies, such as Earthwatch, seemed to attract a wide range of ages and volunteers of both sexes. While I ended my year without a partner, I did come away with a new set of fantastic friends.

The placement agency you choose and your co-volunteers can be major influences in the success and enjoyment of your volunteer vacation. If you still have questions, ask around for suggestions from other volunteer vacationers. What were their experiences with specific agencies and placements? Are any of their recommendations on your short list or did they suggest an agency that sounds like a good fit for you?

Notes

5 When...

Volunteer vacations can range from a week to two years. For many people, the main determinant for selecting a particular volunteer placement is *when* they can take their vacation. They may have to look for opportunities that fit a work schedule or accommodate family plans. For volunteers who are between school and career or enjoying retirement, the timing of a volunteer vacation likely plays less of a role.

When Can You Go and How Much Time Do You Have?

Once you are clear about the general timeframe for your vacation, you can look at specific scheduling issues. Here are important issues to consider:

Time zones and hemisphere – When you travel across time zones and hemispheres, you may experience jetlag upon arrival. One of the best ways to minimize the negative effects of jetlag is to be prepared for it and understand how it might affect you. If your schedule and destination is such that your first day of vacation might be lost due to sleep deprivation, consider arriving a day or two before you begin work to acclimate yourself and let your body adjust. Hydration and plenty of rest can also help you feel energized and ready to work. (See the Time Zones Map in Chapter 29.)

Project start date – Some agency brochures list exact start and end dates for volunteer duties. Other agencies have a flexible schedule, and you can begin your placement at any time. It is usually wise to be in the country at least one day in advance of the start of the project. This is especially important if your placement requires additional travel to the site.

> ### A Few Extra Days
>
> Whenever possible, adding travel days on both sides of your volunteer placement dates is recommended. It might prevent you from arriving late if you experience delays. Otherwise, it allows you time to acclimate to your new location and time zone.

Crossing the Date Line – If you select a project for which you have to cross the International Date Line and you will lose or gain a day to get there, be sure to factor that in when buying your airline tickets. You do not want to arrive a day late and find that the group has moved on without you!

> ### The International Date Line
>
> When crossing the International Date Line, your airline ticket should clearly state your arrival date at your destination with an indication such as +1 or -1 or next day. Speak to your ticketing agent before you purchase to make sure you understand any potentially confusing arrival or departure dates.

Program availability – Not all programs are available year round, and some projects may only be offered quarterly or even every other year. Check with your volunteer agency.

Shoulder Season – If you have the luxury of traveling during off-peak seasons, called "shoulder seasons," you may be pleasantly surprised. Shoulder season travel may offer you reduced rates on airfare and hotels, and possibly even reduced agency placement fees. It usually also means fewer tourists at your destinations.

Returning to Work – If you are taking time off work for your vacation, if possible, do not plan any big meetings immediately after you return. You may want a few days to settle back into the office routine or may be thankful you have a day or two of no specific plans in case your flight is delayed and you're late returning to work.

Side Trips or Mini-Vacations

Do you have sufficient time to include a little vacationing before or after your volunteer work? I hope so! In addition, or instead, you may have a small amount of time off during your volunteer work. The volunteer agency literature should indicate your work and time-off schedule.

Local transportation may not be readily available for side trips, so if you plan to do some serious vacationing around your volunteer work, consider adding days before or *after* your volunteer commitment.

Liz, a volunteer I worked with in Thailand, advises taking a small excursion *after* your volunteer work ends. "It allows you something to look forward to when the post-volunteer blues set in and you don't want to go home just yet!"

A Single Day

Be aware, especially if you are planning to volunteer for only a week or two, that it's common to receive only a single day or partial day off during a two-week volunteer placement.

Plan Ahead to Have Fun

When I was in Thailand on a placement with Earthwatch, some of the volunteers and I decided to visit Angkor Wat in Cambodia following our volunteer work. We began our discussions via email before we arrived and solidified our air, hotel, and private guide reservations during our volunteer placement. It was fortunate we waited to make our arrangements until we were in the area, as we met people who had just taken the same trip to Cambodia so we got up-to-date advice.

In the Notes space, you can explore your options for desired vacations offered at different times of the year. If you have two different locations or types of work you would like to investigate, consider exploring the details of both and see if one rises to the top as your first choice. Another option is to mind map several destinations.

Notes

Notes

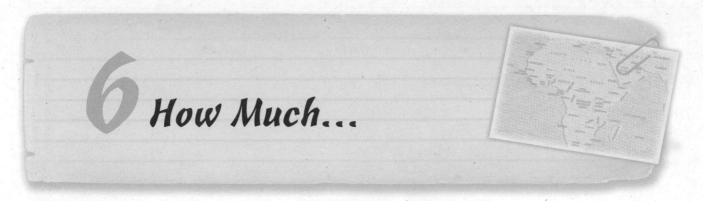

6 How Much...

A volunteer vacation has associated costs, just like other vacations. For this type of vacation, the costs are incurred either by the volunteer placement agency, the volunteer, or both.

What Does It Cost to Use a Placement Agency?

Volunteers will pay a fee to a placement agency to cover certain operating costs incurred both before and during the volunteer work. What the volunteer placement fee covers can vary depending on the particular agency's mission, how it is organized, and the type of volunteer work selected. I recommend verifying the exact expenses covered in the fee paid to your volunteer placement agency.

Most, if not all, of the following expenses are generally covered in the volunteer placement fee:

- Pre-trip literature
- Airport pick-up and drop-off
- Local ground transportation other than the above
- Lodging and meals
- On-the-job training
- Health insurance while a volunteer on the work site
- A donation to support the local or foreign-based project

Plan Ahead for Ground Transportation

During my year away, **sometimes** I was picked up and dropped off at the airport. With other placements, I was picked up at the airport, but I had to pay for my own transportation back to the airport. In these cases, I was always given recommendations for transportation options and help getting to the pick-up point. Please read your brochures and pre-trip literature carefully so you are aware of these travel logistics and can plan ahead.

In my travels, I used six different agencies. The placement fee for a two-week project ranged from $700 to $1,000 for non-U.S. agencies and $2,000 to $2,400 for U.S. nonprofits.

Remember: Depending on your tax profile, you may be able to write off a sizable portion of the U.S. nonprofit agencies' fees, which can bring the foreign and U.S. fees into close alignment.

Researching Placement Costs

When comparing agencies that offer volunteer placements in similar locales, make sure you are comparing apples to apples. Look at the length of volunteer work in days, lodgings, local transportation, insurance, support, and so on. When you find one that is considerably cheaper than others, look deeper. What is *not* included in the less expensive option?

When is the Money Due?

Generally, unless you are within 90 days of departure, your placement fee is not payable all at once. Most often you can reserve your space on a specific trip with a deposit of approximately 25 percent of the placement fee. The balance is usually due to the volunteer placement agency 90 days before the start of the volunteer placement.

Savings Plans

Earthwatch offers prospective volunteers the opportunity to set up an "expedition fund," a kind of savings plan, for up to two years before departure. You or family and friends can make deposits to the account, so when it is time to pay for your placement fee, the funds are available. An added bonus is that all donors to your fund will receive a letter from Earthwatch confirming the tax deductibility of their donations.

You might consider the cost difference between international and domestic placements. Some volunteer placement agencies, such as Global Volunteers and Earthwatch, offer not only international projects, but also projects in the United States, Mexico, and Canada. The price for North American placements may be only two-thirds the cost of international placements.

Same Work – Different Agencies – Different Costs

I had four placements working with wildlife, for which volunteers arrived through different channels. While I was placed through agencies such as I-to-I and Enkosini, my co-volunteers were placed by Green Volunteers, WWOOF, and AVIVA. Some volunteers paid less for the placement than I did. You may want to compare costs if you find that several agencies place volunteers at the same site.

Out-of-Pocket Expenses

Similar to vacationing at an all-inclusive resort, you will have to pay some out-of-pocket expenses besides your initial fee. These generally include:

- Airfare
- Passport/Visa
- Vaccinations
- Pre- and/or post-volunteer work vacations
- Recreation
- Alcohol, snacks, and meals when not volunteering
- Transportation for after-hours activities

To further research a volunteer placement based on the cost, you can:

- Go to **www.idealist.org**.
- Search the Internet using the words "no cost or low cost volunteer work" and the country you want to visit.
- Read books that break down volunteer options by price: For example, *Volunteer Vacations: Short-Term Adventures That Will Benefit You and Others* by Bill McMillon, or *Green Volunteers* by We Care Guides.

Would You Lead?

If you find a volunteer placement agency that you really like and you enjoy working with volunteers, ask if the agency needs people to help lead trips. By leading a trip, your expenses may be covered. Another possible scenario to reduce your cost is to see if you would receive a discount for coordinating a group of volunteers to go on a specific trip.

Many factors determine how much you spend on a volunteer vacation: domestic or international, type of work, length of time, agency selected, and so forth. Comparing the cost of a traditional versus a volunteer vacation, you will probably find, as I did, that the up-front costs are often equal. However, when you consider the possible tax advantages, the heart factor, and the potential educational benefits, you may find a volunteer vacation is a better option than a traditional one, both monetarily and emotionally.

Notes

Part Two: 8 to 6 Months Before You Leave

After Part Two, you will have:

- ❑ Completed Chapters 7 to 10
- ❑ Paid a deposit to your volunteer placement agency
- ❑ Evaluated your health needs, including insurance coverage while out of country
- ❑ Begun vaccinations and determined what prescriptions to take
- ❑ Applied for or updated your passport
- ❑ Researched if you need a visa
- ❑ Considered options for flights and ground transportation
- ❑ Gathered your support team for home logistics

7 Health Topics...

You have determined your destination; now it is time to investigate health topics such as vaccinations, prescriptions, first aid kit, insurance, and emergency health care.

Information About Vaccinations

If you will be traveling to a foreign country and visiting a location outside a major metropolitan area, you will likely need a few vaccinations. Here are several places to search for what you will need based on your destination.

Private Practitioner – Consider beginning here, especially for common vaccinations, as they may be covered by your current health insurance. Flu, measles, tetanus, and hepatitis injections should be available from your family doctor.

Local Travel Clinic – This can be the best resource for up-to-date news on health issues around the world. This includes advice on your first aid kit, vaccinations, prescriptions, travel advisories, and appropriate antimalarial and altitude medications, including side effects. (If you have several clinics in your area, shop around, as prices can vary and availability of some vaccines may be limited.)

Full Coverage

Be aware: Some vaccination regimes, such as Hepatitis B, can take up to six months for full coverage. It is best to start your research early.

Center for Disease Control – You may find that **www.cdc.gov** has more information than you may want concerning diseases and health issues around the world. However, the CDC is an excellent resource for in-depth information.

Volunteer Agency Information Packet – The agencies are *very* aware of what is going on at the locale where your volunteer work is set.

Travel Clinics in Foreign Countries –The clinic may also be able to help with vaccinations if you left home without them or need to complete a vaccination series. (Note: Vaccinations can be important. If at all possible, it is best *not* to leave home without them.)

Clinics Abroad

During a long trip, I used the services of travel clinics in both Australia and New Zealand for additional vaccinations and medications. I found them to be efficient, knowledgeable, and less expensive than similar clinics in the United States.

Health-Related Items You *Must* Carry

Especially important when traveling abroad is having your health records up to date and close at hand. It is recommended that you *always* carry these items:

Vaccination Record – As you land in a foreign country, immigration officials will want to see your passport and at times, your vaccination record. For instance, if you have previously visited a country where a yellow fever vaccination is required and your vaccination record is not current, you could be denied entry, including back into the United States.

List of Prescriptions on Your Physician's Stationery – If you will be carrying multiple prescriptions, immigration officials may want to make sure they are for your personal use. A safeguard is to make sure each prescription clearly states your name, your physician's name, and the chemical name of the drug, not just its trade or generic name.

Prescribed Medications – Remember to always travel with prescribed medications in their original containers. Ask your pharmacist for the smallest bottle possible with your label attached. This way, you will only take what you need for your trip and a few extras just in case.

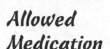

Allowed Medication

Some countries restrict the type of medications travelers can bring into the country. Ask the travel clinic about possible restrictions for your regular prescribed medications.

First Aid Kit – The type of volunteer work you will do can determine what you need to put in your first aid kit. (Go to page 51 for a partial list of first aid supplies.) For example, in some locations, you may need bandaging supplies while in others, you may need rehydration salts. If you will be based in a city with plenty of resources, you may be able to carry a very small first aid kit. However, if you are based in a remote location without pharmacies nearby, you may feel more comfortable carrying a complete kit.

Small But Mighty

I suggest making your first-aid kit small but powerful. For example, it is not necessary to carry an entire bottle of medication when small "blister packs" clearly listing the contents are available. If you run out during your trip and you are in or near a city, you can usually find pharmacies with over-the-counter name brand drugs or equivalents.

Special Supplies – Most travelers have a few items that they feel are always necessary when they travel. The most common are extra eyeglasses (both reading and sun), contact lens solutions, allergy medications, and feminine products. For my comfort, I always carry emergency dental supplies such as dental wax.

Insurance

Health insurance coverage is usually included in the fee you paid to the placement agency while doing your volunteer work. However, being covered by health insurance while away from the work site is a common concern. To find out about your coverage, you can:

- Contact your current health insurance provider to determine if you have coverage when out of the country. Ask: "Will you cover me under all circumstances, even if I participate in an extreme sport such as bungee jumping?" If the answer is no—even if you are not planning on doing anything extreme to begin with, you may change your mind during your trip. Therefore, obtaining supplemental health insurance may be wise.

- Ask the volunteer agency what its standard health insurance covers for a volunteer and for how long. You may be able to extend its coverage for a few days before or after the volunteer placement and/or increase the level of coverage for a few additional dollars.

Who Pays?

If you have a health issue come up during your trip, duplication of coverage for medical issues could cause confusion. Please speak to your insurance agent and the volunteer agency to determine which policy will take precedence while you're working as a volunteer or vacationing out of the country.

Many travel insurance agencies also offer emergency medical services, medical evacuation, and repatriation coverage. Ask your volunteer agency for names of insurance agencies it uses or recommends. (See "Resources" for listing of insurance agencies – travel.)

Are You in Shape Physically?

Depending on the type of volunteer work you will take on, you may need to be fit and ready. For example, if you will be hiking and/or carrying equipment, consider beginning a training program early so you are in good shape when you arrive. If you will be doing special activities such as scuba diving, you may want to take a refresher course to make sure you're prepared.

The Big D!

If you come down with diarrhea while in a foreign locale, the local pharmacists probably have the most effective prescription for dealing with the local bugs. The entertaining part of the exercise will be describing the exact nature of your complaint. Don't worry; these pharmacists are probably used to working with clients from other countries that have similar needs.

Do not delay or be afraid to tell your local volunteer coordinator if you become ill during your international volunteer work. They usually have been to the area before and know exactly where to take you for assistance.

The following page is for you to record the names of the vaccinations, prescriptions, and medications you found you will need during your research.

Health Topic Status List

Regular Prescriptions

_____

_____

Trip-Specific Prescriptions

_____

_____

Over-the-Counter Medications

_____

_____

Suggested Vaccinations	Country	Current	Still Need

Notes

8 *Passport and Visa*

Wherever you go, *you will need a passport*. You may also need a visa, depending on the country(ies) you visit and the length of your stay. If you have a passport, now is the time to make sure it is current. If you do not have one, I recommended you apply for it right away; it can take up to six months to be issued unless you want to pay extra for express processing.

Applying for a U.S. Passport

What do you need before you apply for your first passport? In addition to the application found at **www.travel.state. gov/passport/** the usual documentation includes your birth certificate and a passport photo. I suggest previewing the application very carefully to make sure you have all the necessary information at hand for a successful first-time submission.

Passport Photo

Most pharmacies, photo-processing shops, and travel stores offer "while-you-wait" passport photos. Consider purchasing a few extra photos that you may need for visa applications.

Application and Processing Time

Be aware that processing passports may take anywhere from two weeks to six months even if all the paperwork is in order and it's not high travel season. Only expect a response in two weeks if you expedite the service with additional costs for express shipping. It's best to ask postal service workers for an estimated processing time.

> ### Your First Passport
>
> If you are applying for an initial passport, *you must submit the application in person* at a U.S. Postal Service location that processes passports. Check **www.USPS.com** to locate the closest office that provides this service.

Note: U.S. passports are good for 10 years if you are over 16 years of age.

Renewing Your Passport

Passport renewals may be handled through the mail, providing your passport did not expire within the last 15 years. If your passport did expire more than 15 years ago, you will need to start the process from scratch, just like a first-time applicant.

Number of Pages

The standard U.S. passport comes with 24 pages. If you already have a passport but have only a few blank pages left, or if you are a first-time applicant expecting to travel extensively, you can request additional pages. There is no fee for this service, but it does take time so don't wait until you get close to your departure date. Send off your passport and the request for extra pages early.

Expiration Date

As you enter their country, most immigration officials want to make sure your passport will not expire within the next six months. Specifically, they want to avoid having people enter the country, have their passports expire, and then not be able to return to their home country.

If your passport is due to expire less than 6 months of your arrival into the country, officials may not allow you to enter.

Applying for a Foreign Visa

With most agencies, when you enter a country for a volunteer vacation, you usually enter as a **tourist**. Most countries automatically grant tourist visas, at no charge, for 30 to 90 days. Some countries that require tourists to have a visa will allow you to purchase one as you immigrate into the country.

Some countries and immigration officials do not understand the difference between volunteer work and paid work. If you mention that you are "working," they may insist you get a business visa. That procedure can be costly and time consuming, and it may delay your arrival at your volunteer work site. If asked at immigration the purpose of your trip, say you are vacationing, which is true.

A Visa While You Wait

In the middle of a trip to Thailand, I joined a group of fellow volunteers on a side trip to Cambodia. Upon arrival at the airport in Siem Reap, I purchased my Cambodian visa by filling out a visa application, supplying two passport photos, and paying a U.S. $40 fee in cash. This is why I always bring extra passport photos and cash in U.S. dollars for impromptu side trips.

Presenting Your Visa Upon Arrival

For some countries, you *must* arrive with a visa in your passport. If this is the case, you may have to send your passport to the embassy or consulate of that country along with photos, the fee, and an application form. Visa processing can take up to a month; therefore, *plan in advance*. Your volunteer agency will tell you when and how to apply if a visa is needed for the country where you are being placed.

How Long Will You Stay?

For those countries that require a physical visa as you arrive, make sure to determine the length of time you plan to stay in the country. If you think you might need to extend your stay, get a visa with extended time well before you travel.

Australia requires you to have a visa no matter the length or nature of your visit and makes it easy to obtain one. Simply apply for your visa online at **www.immi.gov.au**.

Prepare at Home or Pay More Later

I planned to stay in Australia for three months, applied for a visa, and received it electronically for under $20 U.S. before I left on my trip. During my time in Australia, my plans changed and I needed to stay an additional month. When I went to the immigration office in Sydney to complete the visa extension application, the fee was A$200. When I asked why the price was so much higher, they said because I was already in the country.

Hold On to Your Receipts

What looks like a non-descript receipt that you received at immigration may actually be your temporary tourist visa. Keep any form or stamped receipt that you receive at immigration in your passport at all times while in the country.

For many travelers, once you've obtained your U.S. passport, you don't have to think about it for 10 years. When it is not in use, I suggest you keep your passport safe but readily available. You want to be ready for that impromptu trip when offered.

If you travel extensively, you already know it pays to think ahead by making sure you have sufficient pages available before a major trip. In the space provided, you can make notes about the status of your passport and any visas needed.

MY PASSPORT EXPIRES _____   # PAGES OPEN _____

Visas Needed	Country	Cost	Date Applied

Notes

9 Transportation

Next to the fee you paid to the volunteer placement agency, air transportation can be the largest, or second largest, expense for your trip. There are ways to reduce your costs, even in these times of high airfares.

Reducing Flight Costs

Use frequent flyer miles – If you are a long-term planner, you can use your accumulated air miles to book your flight. You could also ask family and friends to gift you their frequent flyer miles (all within one family of airlines, of course). There will likely be a service fee to use your miles, and the airlines may add fuel surcharges on top of the miles used. When using miles, also be sure to check for blackout dates and monitor the economic status of your airline before you book your flight. It is recommended you get an estimate of your costs both for paying the fare and by using miles, and then see which one is better for you.

Plan weekday departures – Once you have researched a tentative itinerary, check with your ticketing agent to see if a lower fare is available if you depart on a specific day of the week. Traditionally, airfares are lower for a Tuesday or Wednesday departure.

Fly on a partner airline – You may have experienced being ticketed for a trip on one airline and find yourself on a plane from one of their mileage partners. Find out if more than one air partner serves your destination and if there is a cost difference depending on the carrier.

Plan Ahead

If you are using frequent flyer miles, I suggest you begin your research and possibly book your flight *at least six to eight months before* departure, especially if you will need international flights.

How About a Partner?

When I was looking at flights from Los Angeles to Auckland, both United Airlines and Air New Zealand flew the route. Even though they were both in the Star Alliance system, by booking on Air New Zealand, I saved $300 on the final ticket.

Fly separately to a U.S. coastal city – At times, a roundtrip ticket from one of the U.S. coastal city airports (New York, Washington Dulles, LAX, or San Francisco) to an international destination is considerably cheaper than from an internal city, such as Denver or Nashville. By making two round-trip reservations, one to the coastal city and another one for the international flight, you may be able to save some money.

Doubled Change Fees

Reminder: when making non-connected reservations, if you have to change one flight, you will need to change both, which can mean double change fees. Also remember, if your first flight is delayed, there is no guarantee the second flight will wait for you.

Purchase changeable tickets – This is *not* the least expensive option; in fact, they may cost double the regular fare for your ticket. But if you think you might need to change your itinerary, consider spending more money up front. This type of ticket can offer greater flexibility than non-refundable tickets, plus any possible changes have already been paid for. When considering this type of ticket, research and calculate what the changes fees will be to make a change to a standard ticket, and then see which option is better for your trip.

Purchase around-the-world tickets – If your volunteer vacation will take you to more than one foreign country, this might be a great option for you. There are two options to consider for these tickets.

> **Package combinations with fixed prices** – The AirTreks representative explained that these tickets are on certain groups of airlines and offer pre-package specific destinations and combination of routes for a fixed price. The package may come with restrictions on routes, limited stopovers, no backtracking, and limited overland travel. If, however, one of these packages fit your plans, it may be a good option for you.

> **Package of sequential one-way airline tickets** – These tickets allow travelers to follow a general westerly or easterly direction, but with more leniency. Traditionally, these tickets allow you to pick your cities and, once selected, they are set. However, you can change your flight dates, usually without additional penalty fees. These tickets aren't restrictive if you want to backtrack. Another bonus is that you don't have to start and stop in the same city, and they don't tend to restrict the airlines you use.

In general, I've found that buying around-the-world tickets is cheaper than purchasing several individual roundtrips to international destinations.

Around the World

If you are flying to India from the United States, why not buy an around-the-world ticket and add a few more cities to your trip? Perhaps you can break up your journey in Bangkok so you can begin to acclimate to the jetlag. Then, after your volunteer work, reward yourself with some well-earned recreation in a European country before you fly home.

Use in-country discount airlines – Once you are in the foreign country, if you need additional local flights, ask around for discount airlines. A few of these include Ryan Air (Europe), Kululu (South Africa), and Virgin Blue (Australia). While you may be able to book these in-country flights while you are still in the U.S., if your itinerary is flexible, you may prefer to wait until you arrive to purchase flights within the country and you're sure of your schedule. The representative from AirTreks advises that some in-country airfares (Vietnam and Argentina) are intended for their citizens only and are not available to foreign travelers. I also found that at times, it was difficult for me to purchase tickets on-line for an in-country or discount airline, if I was not on the same continent at the time I was making the purchase.

In-Country Flights

I had purchased an around-the-world ticket that got me to my starting city in each country. When I needed in-country flights in South Africa, I was surprised to find that the airline I arrived on affected my choice of flights within the country. I arrived on Cathay Pacific, an American Airline partner. The major airline in the country, South African Airline, operates within the United Airlines network. Because I had arrived via a different network, I was not eligible to buy a package deal for flights within South Africa on South African Airlines.

Trip Insurance

In "Resources," you will see a list of several agencies that specialize in various insurances dealing with travel. They insure against trip cancellations or delays, medical insurance/evacuation, lost luggage, and, at times, air default coverage. When you consider the entire cost of your volunteer trip, having one or several of these insurance policies may give you peace of mind.

When to Buy Insurances for the Trip?

Typically, you are required to purchase your various travel insurance policies at the time you purchase your airline tickets. While you may be able to purchase these after you have been ticketed, any preexisting medical conditions will not be covered. Also, if you are buying trip cancellation insurance after you are ticketed, know that you will be paying the same price for fewer days of coverage.

Ground Transportation

Depending on your locale and length of stay, the options for ground transportation may vary considerably. Once you have finalized your itinerary, you're ready to find the transportation resources. Reading the literature carefully ahead of time can help you sort through the options and make decisions for your trip.

While Volunteering – Some volunteer vacations will cover the costs for picking you up as well as any local transportation you will need during your trip. Others may require you to make your own arrangements.

Your transportation from the airport to either the pickup point or the actual volunteer location may be covered within your placement fee. If not, check with the agency for suggestions on how to get to the pickup location.

Generally, all ground transportation during the time you're *working as a volunteer* is covered unless specifically excluded. Check with your volunteer agency on the most efficient and economical ground transportation for your trip.

While Vacationing – If you want to travel while you're away, many countries provide fantastic rail and bus networks. Guidebooks explain excellent resources for all in-country transportation options, such as trains, buses, shuttles, rental cars, and taxis—including what you'll need to do to get from the airport to your first or last hotel.

My European Guru

For European destinations, I suggest checking out Rick Steves' website, **www.ricksteves.com**, to find prices, routes, and schedules for tours and rail transportation.

Remember, if you're traveling in Europe, rail passes such as Britrail and Eurail must be purchased before you leave the United States. If you plan to use local trains, you may be better off purchasing your tickets after you arrive in the country and have a firm itinerary.

With the Internet all around us, it can be easy to think that, with enough time and effort, you can find the best deal for your trip, and perhaps you can. However, a representative from AirTreks offers this advice:

"Simple roundtrips can be handled online and are usually your cheapest option. More complex trips, or trips that are difficult to book online, should be turned over to a travel agent. Airlines have eliminated commissions to travel agents, so you may pay more than the face value of the ticket to use one. But if the agent finds a cheaper way to construct your fare and offers you peace of mind, a small service fee should be worth it."

Notes

10 Preparing to Be Away from Home

You will be able to take off with only adventure on your mind if you make sure that all of your domestic issues are in order: legal, financial, house care, car storage, pet and plant care, and more. As I have found, these issues can take on a special importance if you are single with no family in the vicinity.

Most importantly, you want to make sure you have discussed your wishes for your home and yourself with family and friends *before* you leave for the airport, even if you will be away for only two weeks.

Legal Issues

When traveling overseas, make sure you have people in the U.S. who know your wishes. To ensure this, fill out and properly file your—

- Will
- Living will
- Durable power of attorney
- Medical power of attorney

Tell Everyone!

As soon as you know you want to take a volunteer vacation, tell your most supportive friends and family. They can help you stay on track and will begin to brainstorm things that will help you. You will want a strong support network, or an "A Team," while you are away to make sure things at home remain calm. Those in your "A Team" are usually so excited about your trip, they may offer to help with car storage, shuttle you to the airport, or plant and pet sit while you are away.

It is recommended to place copies of these documents in safekeeping with a family member, a close friend, an attorney, or your accountant.

Paying Bills

Most likely, you have bills to take care of while you are away. You will want to decide—

- Who will pay your bills or mail postdated payments for you
- Whether you want to pay your bills in advance
- If you will use the Internet to pay your bills online while away

If you have a person handling your accounts, find out what the bank requires for your proxy to access your bank accounts with your authorization.

Share Your Itinerary

In addition to extra printed copies of your itinerary, passport, and tickets that you will carry with you, make sure to leave several copies of the above mentioned documents along with your contact information list with family members or friends. Your contact information list should include their phone numbers and email addresses. It's especially important to include the contact information for your volunteer placement agency.

While I know you want to get away from your regular job for a while, it's best to give people at work your information and take work phone numbers with you. If you are unavoidably detained returning to the U.S., these numbers will make it easy to keep your employer informed.

Your Home and Possessions

Who will care for your home and possessions while you are away? What do you want these caregivers to do for you? Consider—

- Who will check on your house if there is inclement weather or power outages
- Who will make your home look lived in and how (e.g., collecting mail, gathering newspapers, adjusting drapes, etc.)
- Who will water your plants and/or grass
- If you will hire a house sitter
- What actions you will authorize this person to take on your behalf
- If you want your mail and newspaper held until you return
- If you want your lights put on a timer system
- Where you will park your car

Caring for Your Pets

What about your pets? Think about if they will—

- Be boarded or stay in your home
- Stay with a family member or friend
- Be taken care of by a pet sitter who visits daily or stays in your home

It is also wise to alert your vet about your trip, and authorize him or her to work with your pet sitter in case of medical emergencies.

Special Events and Deadlines

Life goes on, even when you are on a volunteer vacation. Before your trip, decide how you will keep track of your home life and events when you are away. Think about—

- Birthdays and anniversaries
- Important deadlines such as school and sports teams enrollment
- Elections

If any of these items can't be handled before you leave, find someone to take care of them for you.

What other issues have not been covered regarding your home life? Jot down ideas, duties, and a list of people who potentially might agree to assist you.

Take a Breath

By now, you have many of the major decisions behind you. Well done! The time spent may have seemed like a lot, but it will pay off in the long run. When you have done this type of in-depth research at least once, your next trips become much easier. (I'm sure you know by now you probably have more than one volunteer vacation trip in your future!)

But for now, I invite you to take a slow, deep breath and consider what you have accomplished. Take a day off to celebrate your preparations to date. Then you can move on to PART THREE.

Part Three: 3 Months to 1 Month Before You Leave

After Part Three, you will have:

- ❑ Read Chapters 11 and 12
- ❑ Paid the volunteer agency the balance due on your placement fee
- ❑ Applied for needed visas
- ❑ Completed the balance of your travel arrangements
- ❑ Made lodging reservation(s)
- ❑ Evaluated vacation and sightseeing opportunities
- ❑ Researched the culture you will be entering

11 Lodging

This chapter addresses three types of lodgings: where you will stay (1) during your volunteer placement, (2) on your first and last night in the country, and (3) after your volunteer work ends and during your vacation.

Lodging While Volunteering

Your lodging and food is usually included as part of your volunteer work. If housing is not included, ask your volunteer agency for a list of recommended lodgings in the area.

Lodging for First and Last Night in the Country

Even with the best-laid plans, planes can be delayed. Arriving in the wee hours of the morning after a long flight is not the best time to look for lodgings in a foreign country. Consider that making first night hotel reservations gives you an excellent safety net. Having last night reservations will also make your departure easier.

Here are some suggestions for selecting the best lodging for your trip:

Close to the airport – Making reservations for lodging near the airport allows for a comfortable start and end to your volunteer vacation.

Close to a site of interest – If you arrive a few days early, think about choosing a hotel close to local sites of interest to cut down on transportation time and costs.

At the volunteer pickup location – If your volunteer pickup location is a hotel, by staying there you may easily and quickly meet the other volunteers and can plan excursions with them. Often, the volunteer placement agency negotiates a discounted group rate for volunteers who arrive early or leave late.

Lodging While Vacationing

Occasionally, your flight/train/bus is delayed and you don't reach your vacation destination city until after the tourist bureau or housing desk at the airport or terminal is closed. Or you might arrive during a major school holiday or when a huge festival is in full swing, making it difficult to search for a room. To be prepared, consider these options:

Making first and last night hotel reservations in any city you visit close to the airport or terminal. You don't want to miss one minute of your well-deserved vacation locating a hotel due to a transportation delay. Making your last night reservation close to the airport, especially if you have an early morning flight, allows you to get to the airport with a minimum of effort.

Resevations Are Your Friend!

I had two experiences while vacationing in New Zealand, when I appreciated having reservations my first night in a city. The first time, my train was delayed by more than six hours and I arrived in Wellington well after midnight. The second time was during a minor flood and our bus was stranded overnight four hours away from my destination.

Luckily, I had reservations in both instances and called ahead to alert my lodging hosts of the delay. Had I not made reservations, I would have arrived disheveled, exhausted, and stressed about where to stay.

House sitting – If you're staying in an area for an extended period, check out possible house sitting opportunities. (See "Resources" for websites about house sitting.)

Youth hostels – Youth hostels are no longer just a haven for the under-30s toting backpacks. Networks of hostels cater to all travelers who desire economy and basic accommodations.

Why I Love the YHA!

I was pleasantly surprised by the accommodations offered by the YHA Youth Hostels at **www.hihostels.com** in New Zealand, Australia, and South Africa. I went through a global network that offered a wide range of options including single, double, dorm, or family rooms. Some locations had restaurants and in-room TVs. All offered self-service laundry, Internet access, communal cooking and dining areas, and an ever-shifting clientele from around the world, ranging in age from 17 to 75.

Across the board, they were clean, safe, and conveniently located, and provided a wealth of information of where to go and what to do locally.

By being a part of a hostel network, most of the individual hostels offered discounts on multiple-night stays and many had on-site travel agents. Easily, it was the best NZ $40 I spent while traveling.

Where to lodge is a highly personal decision. Depending on your volunteer placement, you may need a little pampering afterward. Conversely, you may be eager to get your backpack and sleeping bag out of storage and head for the wilds. Knowing your preferences and mapping them in advance can be the icing on the cake for your amazing volunteer vacation.

Notes

12 Research Your Vacation and the Local Culture

You may have specifically picked a region of the world that is very different from where you live. You have dreamed and imagined what it will be like and how you will react. The reality of your chosen destination can seem especially foreign if you arrive jetlagged and exhausted.

By doing some research on the culture and society beforehand, you will have a better idea of what to expect and how to prepare yourself.

Vacation Opportunities

Since you are already in the area, you might as well check out the sights *and* sites! Read up before you leave to get an idea of places and things that you would like to experience.

The volunteer agencies do not set up side trips or tours, but they usually have reputable resources to suggest what is available. In addition to services offered by travel agencies and tour groups, for your leisure or vacation activities you may want to consider these options:

Local guides – Hiring "local" guides is often the best way to see the things that really interest you. You get personal attention and have an opportunity to ask more questions from someone who lives within the culture. The guides are happy to share their country, and once they know your interests, they can offer suggestions on what to see.

Group tours – If your time is limited, group tours are an excellent way to see as much as possible in a short amount of time. Remember that tours are traditionally filled with time-crunched travelers like you. Also, when you join a tour, you may not get the opportunity to mingle with the locals or have unlimited time to linger at your favorite sites.

Circulating tour buses – Many of the larger cities offer marvelous several-hour to full-day circulating buses suited for short-term visitors. They are usually inexpensive, have a running commentary on the sites as you drive past, offer hop-on hop-off service, and are a great way to get the feel of your new city. After a day of looking out the window, you may find areas to go back to and explore at your leisure.

Buses

I found that both Madrid and Cape Town offer great circulating bus tours. Check out:
Cape Town, South Africa: City Sight Seeing – **www.citysightseeing.co.za**
Madrid, Spain: Madrid Vision – **www.madridvision.es/en/index.php**

UNESCO Sites

My strongest suggestion is this: When you have the opportunity to visit a United Nations Educational, Scientific and Cultural Organization (UNESCO) site, *do not rush* if you can avoid it! Here is the description from the UNESCO World Heritage website: "The World Heritage List includes 878 properties forming part of the cultural and natural heritage, which the World Heritage Committee considers as having outstanding universal value. These include 679 cultural, 174 natural, and 25 mixed properties in 145 countries." **(whc.unesco.org/en/list)**

A pattern that worked for me was spending my first day at the site with a small group tour learning the lay of the land and checking out the options. Every site had at least one special place that begged for more exploration. When I had the chance for a second day at a site, I would usually go by myself, or hire a local guide, and spend time in an area that was the most breathtaking to me.

Culture Immersion

If you crave to know what it's really like to live, work, and thrive in the county you visit, home stays and local language classes are a great way to dig deep into the culture. There is nothing like a native friend or family to help you understand on a deeper level the culture you are visiting.

Economy

You may be visiting a location that has a markedly different economy than you are used to. Depending on the country you select, the instant you arrive, you may become aware of how different the locale is compared with the U.S.

For example: If you have never been exposed to poverty, at times the apparent misery and the persistence of begging in the street can feel overwhelming. By doing your research, while this kind of situation can still be unsettling, at least you have been alerted to the issue and can mentally prepare for your trip.

Appropriate Behavior, Dress, and Customs

Local dress, behavior, and customs can be some of the most colorful parts of your trip. Knowing what is appropriate behavior and dress in public places while on vacation or during your volunteer work in other countries is important.

"When you travel, remember that a foreign country is not designed to make you feel comfortable. It is designed to make its own people comfortable."

— **Clifton Fadiman,**
American author and radio and TV personality

Some cultures do not approve of smoking or consuming alcoholic beverages. At times, men are allowed to do things that women are not. Some cultures have strict codes about appropriate dress. Research customs in advance, and you can arrive knowing what is appropriate and not inadvertently offend your hosts or embarrass yourself unnecessarily.

Local Language

If you are in a country where English is not commonly spoken or studied widely, you may find that the best on-the-street assistance can come from teenagers, college students, and local universities.

What are the Local Customs?

Guidebooks, your volunteer placement agency, and the consulate for the country you visit can be excellent resources about local customs. They can also answer common questions about tipping, greetings, dress, and general rules of behavior.

Or, with all the social online networking resources available (Journeywoman, LinkedIn, Meetup, etc.), you should be able to find someone in your new city who would be willing to meet you for coffee or a meal to help you get a feel for the culture. If your time is short in one location, the SERVAS organization at **www.servas.org** is a way to spend a few nights with local people who want to help travelers understand their culture.

It's Okay to Ask for Help

Be aware that many cultures seem to have a national mandate that local people drop whatever they are doing and help a lost traveler who asks for assistance. This can feel over the top to Western travelers, but it provides an excellent way to practice language skills in both directions and make new friends.

Body Language, Personal Space, and Smiles

A friendly smile is usually welcome, but in some cultures, it can lead to misunderstandings or unintended promises. Although well intended, your trusting nature and desire to connect may be interpreted as crossing the line.

In some countries, it's common for male or female friends to hold hands in public and kiss upon meeting. It may, however, not be as acceptable for a newcomer being introduced for the first time. In some cultures, a woman traveling alone can be an object of great interest. If you are a woman alone, you may feel more comfortable approaching mature women if you need help or accepting a seat next to a woman instead of a man.

In cultures where personal cars are rare and public transport is extensively used, the local custom of standing very close to someone—sometimes amazingly close—may be uncomfortable to the Western traveler. You may find that in some cities there are women-only buses or train cars, especially during peak travel times.

Likely one of your main reasons for taking a volunteer vacation is to go to a place that is very unlike home. While there, look for and find the helpful people who exist in every culture, share yourself and your smile, and work to get to know them.

Enjoy your time away as you learn about other people and cultures, even within the ranks of the volunteers. What may surprise you the most is what you learn about yourself!

Notes - Vacation

Notes - Culture

Part Four: 1 Month to 1 Week Before You Leave

After completing Part Four, you will have:

- ❑ Read Chapters 13 to 16

- ❑ Inspected your luggage for sturdiness, needed repairs, etc.

- ❑ Prepared what you will pack

- ❑ Decided what money you will carry and how you will carry it

- ❑ Determined how you will stay connected to friends at home

- ❑ Developed your expense tracking system to use on the road

- ❑ Investigated the issues of staying in touch while on the road and after returning home.

13 Deciding What to Pack

When thinking about what to take on your trip, you may want to consider these words from French pilot and author **Antoine de Saint-Exupery**: *"He who would travel happily must travel light."*

Preparing for Packing

Consider limiting the clothes you bring. I found what worked for me for a two-week volunteer vacation was three sets of work clothes and one set of nice clothes that all coordinated. I chose quick-dry fabrics for when I had to hand launder my clothes—usually daily when volunteering.

Luggage

Your volunteer work will determine the type of luggage you bring. Consider that wheeled luggage is not necessarily an asset on cobblestones or on rutted dirt roads in the wild, and plan accordingly.

Quality Counts!

At the suggestion of Elliot Hester, the author mentioned in an earlier suitcase box, I took a Tumi rolling duffle on my yearlong trip. I also brought an Eagle Creek wheelie with an attachable daypack. At times, I found I had too much to carry. Other times, I really appreciated the flexibility of two different-sized wheeled bags.

When I could, I would pack what I needed for two weeks to one month into one bag and store the other with friends or in the luggage storage at the airport. This also helped me stay within the weight limitations for the smaller airlines. (At times, the weight limit was 20 kilograms, or 44 pounds, for checked **and** carry-on bags combined.) When I compared the cost of overweight luggage fees vs. storage, they normally were about the same. However, it was worth it to me, when possible, to have only one piece of luggage and my daypack to handle.

Number of Bags and Weight Limits

Do not wait until you get to the airport to worry about your luggage and weight limits. Weight limits, the amount of luggage, dimensions of each bag allowed, and the fees for flying with them change with the wind. Add to that the different regulations for domestic vs. international flights, and the numbers change again.

If you want to avoid paying any extra luggage fees, the following discussion will give you an idea of bag and weight limits.

The representative at AirTreks offered this information to help you determine how to pack. There are two different methods to determining the baggage restrictions that will apply to you.

Per Piece Rule - On flights to, from, and within North America, baggage is limited by the "piece rule" to two pieces of checked luggage. Contact your airline for the allowable dimensions for each bag. This will also hold true on other flights, *if they are on the same ticket as your North American flights*

Weight Rule - If your other flights are not on the same ticket as your North America flights (i.e., most flights in the rest of the world), baggage is limited by the "weight rule"—a total of 20 Kilograms (44 pounds), total of all pieces, and items including carryon.

Today's airline rules limit each person to a total of 20 kilograms (44 pounds) of luggage, including all checked and carryon items, on most international flights that don't touch the U.S. or Canada.

Carryon baggage is limited to 5 kilograms (11 pounds) and is included in the overall limit of 20 kilograms. Even if you have only a single bag small enough to fit under the seat and weighing less than 20 kilograms, the airline is NOT obligated to let you carry it on. Airline agents can require you to check any bag weighing more than 5 kilograms. Carryon items are included in the overall weight limit, even if they weigh less than 5 kilograms.

Not all airlines strictly enforce luggage limitations. But it's possible to get a strict check-in clerk on any given airline and flight, and you can't count on checking or carrying on more than the rules allow. When you check to see if you are within your free baggage allowance, do as the airline agent will do: Put everything you aren't actually wearing on a scale together, including your purse, shoulder bag, camera, or anything else you plan to carry on or check.

In some cases if you have more bags than are allowed for free, you may be able to pay for the additional pieces and if on a volunteer vacation, those charges may be tax deductible.

Because each airline has its own specifications, it is recommended to pre-check with your airline several weeks in advance, and then one week in advance. Remember, lighter is always better.

How Much Can You Carry?

Make sure you can carry all your luggage by yourself! Some locations on your itinerary may not have elevators or porters.

To save suitcase space and weight, you might be able to leave some of your clothes at home and pick up clothes at your volunteer site. Many veteran volunteers bring clothes they intend to leave at the site for future volunteers. If you are going to a remote area and the program has been operating for several years, ask if there is a supply of clothes left by previous volunteers. Bringing fewer clothes also opens up room in your luggage for gifts.

Here are some ways to reduce the weight of your luggage:

- **Bulk up** - The oldest travel trick is to wear your heaviest clothing or layer the clothing you wear on the plane. Why pack hiking boots that are heavy and take up valuable space?
- **Thrift Shop** - If the volunteer site doesn't have loaner clothes for you to use, once your reach your volunteer pick up city, consider finding a thrift shop nearby to buy what you will need during your volunteer work. You can donate it back when you are through or leave it at the volunteer site.
- **Limit books** - If you are an avid reader, know that many of the volunteer sites have a lending library. You may want to leave the book you bring and pick up a new one for your return trip.
- **Pull out** - Some travelers pull out the chapters they need from their guidebooks and leave the bulk of the book at home.

My Travel Laundromat

When you volunteer, you generally should be able to find laundry facilities on a weekly basis. However, I found it easier at times to do my laundry almost every night. My secret was taking undies, socks, shirts, and pants that could be hand washed and dried overnight. My washing supplies were contained in a Hefty freezer-quality, quart-size, zip-lock bag. It contained a rubber jar opener (for a drain plug), several hanging clothespins, powdered laundry soap, inflatable hangers, and a collapsible clothesline. Shampoo also works for laundry soap in a pinch.

Purchase on Arrival

To keep from adding weight to your luggage, consider traveling with a few small packets of washing powder, such as Woolite, and pick up a larger bag of powdered detergent once you arrive. I also did this with other consumables such as soap, shampoo, deodorant, and toothpaste.

Bring Photographs from Home

A great icebreaker around the world is a photograph. Many volunteer agencies encourage volunteers to bring a few pictures from home to use as conversation starters with children and other volunteers. They can also shoo away the "lonelies" when you are far from family and close friends.

Your Travel Diary

Sometimes in addition to the marvelous pictures you will take on your trip, you will find that the experience requires more detailed exploration. A travel journal may be an essential part of your luggage. In addition to wonderful stories gleaned to turn into the next great travel novel, a journal is an ideal place to write down your emotions, and process unexpected or overwhelming feelings as you go.

Packing Checklist

If you are a veteran traveler, you most likely have a good idea of what you want to pack. If not, I found the following packing list to be comprehensive and helpful. You can modify it to fit your specific trip.

Packing List

BEFORE YOU GO:

__ Passport /ID
__ Visas
__ Visit Doctor/Dentist
__ Insurance Information
__ Traveler's Checks
__ Credit Cards
__ Foreign Currency
__ U.S. Cash
__ Airline Tickets
__ Health Documentation
__ Extra ID
__ Int'l Driver's License
__ Student ID/FHA/Int'l Discount Cards
__ Emergency Information
    (medical, itinerary, relatives)
__ Photocopies of important documents

HEALTH CARE NEEDS:

__ Prescriptions/Birth Control
__ Spare Prescription Glasses
__ First Aid Kit
__ Blister Kit
__ Band Aids
__ Adhesive Tape
__ Compression Bandage
__ Moleskin
__ Antiseptic/Iodine Towellettes
__ Antibiotic Cream
__ Insect Repellent
__ Antihistamine Cream
    (good for itchy insect bites!)
__ Calamine Lotion
__ Sunscreen
__ Lip Balm
__ Tweezers
__ Scissors
__ Aspirin
__ Antihistamine Tablets
__ Antacid
__ Diarrhea Medicine
__ Foot Powder
__ Malaria Pills
__ Vitamins
__ Cold Medicine
__ Laxative
__ Tampons/Pads
__ Water Bottles
__ Water Filter/Iodine Tablets

WASH KIT:

__ Soap
__ Shampoo
__ Deodorant
__ Travel Wash (for clothes)
__ Clothesline
__ Shaving Kit
__ Toothbrush, Paste & Floss
__ Sink Stopper
__ Mirror
__ Towel
__ Contact Lens Preparation
__ Lotions/Skin Creams
__ Hair brush/Comb
__ Toilet Paper
__ Q-Tips
__ Nail Clippers

CLOTHING:
Think light weight, comfortable, quick-drying, abrasion resistant: nylon, polyester & cotton blends

__ Socks (thin cotton, thermal, wool)
__ Gaiters
__ Hat or Visor
__ Gloves/Scarf
__ Comfortable Shorts (2-3 pairs)
__ Skirt
__ Pants (2-3 pair)
__ Belt
__ Shirts (short/long sleeve, Tees, something "dressy")
__ Rainwear
__ Thermal Underwear
__ Sandals, Walking Shoes & Boots
__ Swimsuit
__ Underwear

SOME BIG BASICS:

__ Travel Luggage
__ Suitcase/Travel Pack
__ Fanny Pack
__ Daypack
__ Luggage Keys/Locks
__ Luggage Tags
__ Possession Protectors
__ Money Belt
__ Neck Pouch
__ Pouch for Passport, Tickets & Currency
__ Camera & Accessories
__ Padded Case
__ Tripod Case
__ Extra Film/Memory Cards
__ Lenses
__ Extra Batteries
__ Filmshield (for x-ray protection)

MISCELLANEOUS:

__ Flashlight & Extra Bulbs/Batteries
__ Door Jammer
__ Headlamp
__ Candle
__ Travel Alarm/Watch
__ Sunglasses/Case/Strap
__ Ear Plugs
__ Neck Pillow (for traveling)
__ Voltage Adapter and Converter
__ Modem (tele) Adapter
__ Swiss Army Knife
__ Umbrella
__ Plastic Zip-Lock Bags
__ Sewing Kit/Thread
__ Lighter/Matches
__ Calculator
__ Binoculars
__ Journal
__ Pens
__ Reading Material
__ Travel Guides/Maps
__ Language Books
__ Stuff Sacks
__ Travel Hair Dryer
__ Travel Iron/Steamer

EXTRA GEAR:
Remember, gear can be rented in many tourist areas. Decide if weight or money is more important on your trip.

__ Sport-related Items: Snorkel, diving mask, flippers, climbing harness and boots, etc.

__ Specifics for Climate: Malaria tablets are a necessity in many areas, but don't forget mosquito netting, repellant, coils, or citronella candles.

__ In High Altitude: Make sure your sleeping bag and clothing will keep you warm and dry. Layer clothing. Be sure to acclimatize. You may want to pack altitude sickness medication such as Diamox.

OTHER:

__ Gifts for New Friends
__ Lots of Patience
__ A Good Attitude
__ A Friendly Smile
__ Don't forget to provide for your pets while you are away.

My equation for a happy volunteer is:

Check luggage weight regularly + pack light + carry very little = Happy Volunteer

Checklist was created by Changes In Latitude Travel Store at **www.cil.com**.

14 Money

Money. You are going to need it. Lots of it! Consider this statement from **Susan Heller**, U.S. writer and long-time arts and culture reporter for the *New York Times*:

"On packing: Lay out all your clothes and all your money. Then, take half the clothes and twice the money."

Currencies to Carry with You

While it can be a bother to keep it all sorted, most travelers find it easier to travel with multiple currencies. There are wonderful pocket-sized wallets that have several different zippered compartments. These can be a lifesaver when you are carrying more than one currency.

U.S. Currency - It is generally recommended you carry some U.S. currency, but make sure it is in low denominations ($1, $5 or $10) and each bill is *clean, crisp, untorn, and unmarked*. Some countries prefer our older U.S. currency, as they are not familiar with the newer versions.

Debit Card vs. Credit Cards – Check with your bank to see if there is a difference in the transaction fees for international cash advances on debit cards vs. credit cards. I found exchange rates for debit card transactions were usually lower than credit cards.

Local Currency – You may feel more comfortable arriving with a small amount of the local currency in your hand. That said, many airports allow transactions in the terminals and concourses in U.S. dollars as well as the local currency.

Coins – As soon as you arrive, you may need coins for tips and local transportation on buses or trains. You generally can get change within the airport after you arrive.

 Carrying Local Cash

I usually arrived in a new country with at least U.S. $20 of the local currency. When I landed, I found an ATM or the foreign exchange counter in the airport and took out a larger amount. I would put a small amount in my day wallet, keeping the rest hidden in my money belt.

Traveler's Checks – They are becoming harder to exchange, and usually require that you to go to a bank or large hotel during business hours. However, traveler's checks remain the only form of currency that is replaceable if stolen.

Traveler's Checks Can Be Your Friend

Why will I always travel with a few traveler's checks? On Easter Island, Chile, the preferred currency is the U.S. dollar. I was running low and went to the only ATM on the island to get cash. My card was a Visa on the PLUS system, and the ATM accepted MasterCard on the CIRRUS system. It was late on Saturday and the bank was closed until Monday. I needed cash to pay my guide and eat for another day. Luckily, the Chilean convenience store cashed my traveler's checks. Thank you!

Using ATMs

ATMs are everywhere around the globe, but not always in your exact location or as plentiful as you would like. As stated above, it is wise to carry credit or debit cards on both major systems, CIRRUS and PLUS.

I found that ATMs generally offer excellent exchange rates. It can be amusing to come across ATMs offering two different currencies. For example, ATMs at banks in Peru offered withdrawals in Peruvian Soles or U.S. dollars. Make sure you indicate the currency you want.

Using a Money Belt

Whether worn around your neck or waist, a money belt offers safety for your valuables. The ones made out of cloth or silk tend to be lighter, cooler, and easier to wash. They provide a wonderful way to keep the bulk of your currency safely stored.

Fewer Trips but More Money

It's generally wise to take out larger amounts of money at one time and conceal most of it until needed. Note: Protect yourself! *Always be discrete* when retrieving money in public places.

A Pocket Full of Change

At the end of your visit, you may find you have small-denomination bills or coins that aren't worth exchanging. Look around, because many airports have collection bins for local charities that can turn your coins into resources for those in need.

It's easy to become bewildered when working with local money that looks and feels different from the currency at home. The next chapter discusses how to handle your money and expenses during your trip.

15 *While You Are Away*

You are away on a volunteer vacation, and you want to keep things as simple as possible. Through careful planning, you can make sure your spending stays within your anticipated budget.

While tracking your purchases, tallying daily expenditures, and keeping a list of things to do in a notebook may not sound simple, the time you take to track these things along the way can make your life much easier when you get home.

Keeping Expense Records

If you don't like to do a lot of math in your head, it is easy to create a quick conversion card with common denominations of local currency and the equivalents in U.S. dollars. For example, if you're going to Thailand, your pocketsize conversion chart might look something like this.

U.S. $	Baht		Baht	U.S. $
$0.50	17.52		10	$0.285
$1.00	35.05		20	$0.571
$5.00	175.25		50	$1.42
$10.00	350.50		100	$2.853
$20.00	701		250	$7.133
$50.00	1752.50		500	$14.265
$100.00	3505.00		1000	$28.531
$250.00	8762.50		2000	$57.061
$500.00	17,525		5000	$142.653
$1,000.00	35,050		10,000	$285.307

Exchange rate as of 11/1/08 $1.00= 35.05 Baht

By recording expenses daily and placing your receipts in an envelope or a small zip-lock bag, you can keep your records in order and receipts from escaping. If you are not an avid shopper, customs declarations may not be an issue; nonetheless, you may find it beneficial to keep track of what you spend, not only for gifts but also for potential tax-deductible expenses from your volunteer work. Items to include on your expense record are:

- Date
- Location
- Business name
- Item

- Tax deductible expense?
- Gift
- Amount in local currency
- Amount in U.S. dollars

Envelopes

If you visit multiple countries, one envelope for each country helps keep the purchases, ATM withdrawal slips, or exchange receipts together.

Notes

Paying VAT or GST?

Many countries collect a tax called value added tax (VAT) or a goods and services tax (GST). Most guidebooks have information on these taxes. In addition, as you enter a country, look for more information in the immigration lounges and main terminal. Generally, people in any shop that's frequented by foreign visitors will know about the tax.

If the item purchased comes from an established store, not a street vendor or market, make sure you receive a printed, itemized receipt from the clerk.

Most travelers can receive a refund of these taxes at the airport just before departure if you have the item in your possession and show the itemized receipts. In some countries, you can go through the evaluation process within a few days of departure and pick up your refund at the airport before you leave. It can ease your process if you have the VAT/GST items and the tax receipts in one location for easy access. Either way, I suggest you keep all your receipts handy.

Depending on the dollar amount of your purchases, you should be able to receive the refund in the local currency before you leave. If your anticipated tax refund is a large amount, the refund check might be mailed to your home in U.S. currency.

For information on countries offering VAT refunds for travelers, you can check out: www.foxnomad.com/2008/03/06/how-to-reclaim-taxes-paid-abroad/

It Pays to Know the Rules!

Australia only allows GST refunds on items purchased within the last 30 days of your trip. I bought an expensive item thinking I would be leaving within 30 days. When my plans changed and I ended up staying an additional 30 days, I was not able to receive a refund on my item. (Australian Customs – **www.customs.gov.au/site/page.cfm?u=5347**)

I visited South Africa after Australia, so this time I was ready! South Africa does not have a limitation on when a taxable item is purchased to qualify for a refund. After 90 days in the country, I had a number of items with VAT to be refunded. At the departure terminal at the Johannesburg airport, I proudly handed over my VAT receipts to the inspector and waited, ready to show him any or all of the items I had purchased.

He asked to see a few of the books, which I quickly produced. He wanted to see some of the necklaces I had purchased. No problem. He then looked at one receipt and wanted to know if I still had the ice cream. I said, "No! I don't have the ice cream listed on the receipt!" I *think* he was joking.

I made it through the process and received my VAT refund. I did not receive a VAT refund on my ice cream, though, as I had eaten it!

Keeping in Contact With Home

You are away from home on vacation, potentially far away. There are still ways you can "reach out" from a distance.

Phoning Home

By now you may be aware that the cell phones sold in the U.S. may have limited or non-existent service overseas. While international phone coverage is improving daily, here are ways to make sure you can phone home while abroad:

- **Contact your cell phone provider** and ask about your service while overseas. If your phone has a SIM card (Subscriber Identity Module), make sure your phone is unlocked, and upon arrival, purchase a new SIM card for the country you visit, and keep the one from the U.S. You will have a foreign phone number during your stay, but should avoid high roaming charges. Remember that the instructions may not be in English. Ask for help from the store where you bought the SIM card, and write down the sequence of commands. When you return home, simply reinstall your U.S. SIM card with your old number.

- **Buy a cheap phone** once you're abroad. Alternatively, you may be able to rent one at the airport, if you think it's unlikely you will return to that country. Phones purchased or rented overseas usually have no difficulty connecting with the U.S.

- **Buy phone access cards.** You can purchase phone access cards in nearly every country and use the numbers supplied at pay phones or in hotel rooms to connect with the U.S. You can usually add money or minutes to the cards with a credit card. Some cards offer coverage in additional countries, so you simply top them up when you arrive at your new destination.

- **SKYPE** – If you will be traveling with your computer and expect to have good access to the Internet, SKYPE can help you connect with the U.S. This Internet phone service is free to join for you, your family, and your friends. Depending on where you are, there may be small charge per minute if you are connecting to a landline, but you may find it is less than cell phones or phone cards. To use this service, you will need a headset with a mic, a SKYPE account, and a computer connected to the Internet. For more information, visit **www.skype.com.**

Email Connections

Your friends may be expecting personalized emails about your adventures. If your group of family, friends, and coworkers are satisfied with group emails, YOU ARE LUCKY!

If you are in a city, you should find Internet access everywhere, especially at Internet cafés. The cafés may be filled with local school children playing video games, but the Internet is still accessible to you.

You are almost guaranteed to find plenty of Internet options close to youth hostels and backpackers' lodges. These lodgings tend to be close to the main bus or train terminals as well as major subway junctions.

 One-Stop Service Centers

Look for businesses such as PostNet and Global Gossip for Internet, domestic, and international phone service, local and international mailing, and parcel shipping. You'll find PostNet (**www.Postnet.com**) in 10 countries and Global Gossip (**www. globalgossip.com**) in six countries.

Sending Postcards

Sure, you can text message your friends and send pictures over the Internet, but what if you left the U.S. promising to send postcards? Make it easy on yourself. If you plan to send a card to every person on your Christmas card list, print out mailing labels and take them with you. If you want to send cards to some people from each country you visit, print out a label for them for each country on your itinerary.

International airports tend to have post offices in the terminals. If you know how many postcards you are likely to write, buy the stamps as you arrive and carry them with you. After you have written the cards, you can mail them along the way at your leisure.

Giving and Receiving Gifts

Just as you promised to send postcards, a number of people on your list are likely to expect an exotic gift from you. Heck, any gift! Here's how to simplify your shopping. Compile a list of recipients and mark off their names as you find something to thrill each one.

You may also want to bring small gift items from the U.S. to give to people you meet in your locale.

The Gift Cabinet

Okay, I love to shop, especially in foreign countries. I had a long list of people who deserved gifts, but I did not want to designate who got what. I found it much easier to shop broadly for both men and women along the way. As I returned home, I made a gifting cabinet. Anytime people came over and watched (or lived through) my slides, they could pick something out of the cabinet. They made their own selections, and I was able to relive my trip by telling them about what they had selected and where it was from. My friends loved picking their own gift. I was amazed at times what they selected so I was glad I had bought a large assortment.

In many cultures around the globe, gift giving appears to be a national imperative. This means you may be inundated with gifts, large and small, from people you meet while volunteering. Carrying small thank-you cards allows you to immediately write an acknowledgment for any presents you receive.

What to Do with What You Buy

Not all travelers are major shoppers when on vacation. That being said, most of us return home with at least a few souvenirs. If your luggage was close to the weight limits as you left, how do you plan to get your new "loot" home? Consider these options:

- **Weight allowances** – (See page 49 about bags and weight limits.) Please remember, if you are changing airlines part way home and/or landing in another country, confirm the requirements with *all* of your airlines. Remember, some airlines weigh checked and carry-on luggage. It is best to know in advance how much and how heavy each bag will be before you arrive at the airport.

- **Large/bulky items** – That Maasai spear will look great on your wall in the den, but how are you planning to get it home? Does it collapse into luggage-size pieces? Might it be considered a weapon and therefore suspect? The same goes for the hand-embroidered king-size quilt—it's going to be bulky. How will you get it home? In both these instances, mail may be the answer. Many stores offer shipping services at the time of purchase. This saves you the need to locate a post office or lug your treasure all the way home.

- **Printing mailing labels ahead of time** – If you do plan to shop, consider bringing large, pre-addressed mailing labels with you so you can easily mail packages home.

- **Using the airport post office** – Many international airports have a full-service post office. As long as you give yourself plenty of time, you should be able to clear the tax refund procedure, take your purchases to the airport post office, and still make your plane.

- **Transporting food items** – Check with customs, the guidebooks, and your airlines about the restrictions on food items both coming and going. I found that generally if the product was unopened and clearly showed the contents or manufacturer, it was not a problem. Anything that is open or fresh is best consumed on the plane before you land.

All Mail Is Not Equal

There was no way during my year abroad that (1) I would not shop for gifts or (2) I would be able to carry everything with me and meet weight requirements at the airports. Therefore, I took my FedEx number with me. In Peru, FedEx offices weren't as plentiful as in the U.S. Then, once I found them, I was told NO FOOD ITEMS COULD BE SENT VIA FEDEX (that included coffee, candy, etc.!) Hmm . . . I used the Peruvian National Post Office instead.

As I was ready to leave Thailand, I mailed gifts in six FedEx boxes to various U.S. addresses. Five went through with minor difficulty; the FedEx officers kept asking the recipients what was in the boxes. Because they contained gifts, the recipients did not know. Thankfully, they all were delivered eventually.

My last box was for me and included fabric, puzzles, books, and other small gifts. I was told that U.S. Customs in Alaska held this box because of the fabric. (U.S. Customs officials wanted to know the manufacturer and where I had bought the fabric.) By the time I got news of this, I was in the Cook Islands. After several long distance phone calls to my mail receiver at home and U.S. Customs in Alaska, I asked for the package to be re-directed to New Zealand, where I would visit next. It arrived and I repacked the contents into a regular mailing box and mailed it from the NZ national post office. It arrived with no problems.

From New Zealand on, I used the national post office in every country I visited. I used ground, air, and international overnight services. All 14 packages arrived in the U.S. with no problems.

If you are not an avid shopper, will be gone for only two weeks, or will be in such a remote location that accessing email, post offices, and phones won't be daily occurrences, you may think you will have to bring everyone up to date when you return home. However, on my trip, I found that no matter how remote, I always had a chance to keep in touch with people in the U.S. on at least a weekly basis via phone, Internet, or mail service. It appears to me that the world is getting smaller with the explosion of technology. At times, it also feels like it is getting harder to ever feel truly remote.

Tracking for Customs

Filling out your U.S. customs form will be a lot easier if you keep track of your purchases and whether you mailed them home or are carrying them with you. My understanding from the U.S. Customs office is only items you carry in your luggage are considered for customs allowance. Be sure to confirm this information with the U.S. Customs Service before you leave. Also please remember, packages mailed home may have duty owed when they arrive in the U.S., depending on the value of the contents.

Notes

Returning Home

When you are away on vacation, your mind may be restless with all the things to be done at work and home upon your return. You might be afraid you will forget what you have to do.

Return Duties

Put your mind at rest by keeping a small journal or notebook with you while you travel. If you are ultra-organized, give each type of "return duty" a separate page and jot down thoughts as they come to you both before and during the trip. *Then put the notebook away*, and enjoy your volunteer vacation.

Maintaining Contact with New Friends

I found that international travelers are generally a friendly bunch and love to share information, opinions, and travel advice. You may be amazed at the number of invitations to visit, helpful hints, or entreaties to stay in touch you receive while chatting with fellow volunteers or people you meet along the way.

Consider carrying business cards. They do not need to be expensive. Make sure to include your name and your preferred method of contact. Remember, in today's world of Internet and email, your email address, blog, or website will be more requested than your mailing address.

Inexpensive Business Cards

I used **www.vistaprint.com** to order business cards. If you use the templates and take advantage of the pricing specials offered, you may only have to pay for shipping.

International Friends

I met Erika, a lovely British woman in Thailand during an archaeological dig in February. She was pregnant and expecting her baby in the summer. As England was to be my last stop in December, she invited me to Sheffield. I visited her family just after Christmas and was thrilled to meet her husband, Charlie, and their new daughter, Hana.

In Australia, I was standing on a street corner in Mackay with my map open looking for a certain address. A woman about my age approached and I asked for her assistance. Kaye said she was also from out of town and was visiting her new grandbaby. We spent 40 minutes locating first her destination and then mine; then we parted with each other's contact information. She invited me to look her up when I got back to Sydney. I did, and I spent a great day with her in the northern suburbs. A new friendship was formed after only an initial 40-minute conversation. We still keep in touch via email.

Volunteer Bob has this advice to give about your return: "Keep in mind that after an intense foreign immersion, you may feel alienated from your old life. Your trip was to enhance your life, not detract from it. You saw and experienced things that may be difficult to fully explain. Don't be disappointed if people are a little cool when you begin to share."

Preparing to Be Back Home

You are going home! It is so exciting! You are looking forward to sleeping in your own bed, using your own bathroom, and having a larger number of clothes at your disposal. You will instantly recognize everything you eat, and understand all street signs, conversations, TV, and radio broadcasts.

If you have been away only one to three weeks, these issues may not seem so relevant. But if you've been away for a longer time, you may be acutely aware of the differences between the U.S. and where you have just been.

Here are some things to think about before you get home:

Pace – If you have been fortunate enough to lose the exhausting rush of the modern world while you were away, experiencing the faster pace and volume of activity once you return may be a shock. If possible, give yourself a day or two at home before you expose yourself to the "real world."

Long-term health issues – Even after you return home, keep the records of your trip (where, when) and the medications you took nearby for two or more years. While not common, a medical issue may appear well after your return that was caused by something during your trip. If you have your records handy, they might assist the physician with the diagnosis.

Sharing photographs – You may have hundreds of images to process, print, display, and share, but just remember people back home may not be as interested in every detail as *you* are. Some will be polite and give you plenty of time to expound. Others may have glazed eyes after five minutes and have to leave for an "urgent" meeting. Do not fret. You will find people who are excited about your trip, and they are the people who will appreciate your *entire* slide show.

Reverse Culture Shock

As I approached arrival back in the U.S. after a year abroad, I asked my sister who had recently lived in Thailand for a year, "What can I expect regarding reverse culture shock?" Because I had lived overseas for three years as a child, she recommended the book *The Absentee American,* which describes feelings that frequently surface when returning to the U.S. after an extended journey. (See Suggested Reading in Chapter 27.) She said I might feel vulnerable, assaulted by stimuli, and resemble "a peeled grape."

One thought that proved extremely helpful was this: Other people's lives have gone on while I was away. They are focused on what's been happening in their lives and, while they are "sort of" interested in mine, their own lives hold their main interest. This was very helpful advice when I began to share my stories.

As I returned home, I found everything in the U.S. louder, faster, and more frantic. Major supermarkets unnerved me for a full year after I arrived home because of their vast assortment and abundance. For a multitude of reasons, I'm glad to be back, but I'm also not 100 percent sure that I'm glad I have acclimated again. Sounds like it's time for another international trip!

Notes

Part Five: It is Time to Go!

After Part Five, you will have:

- ❑ Done your preliminary packing
- ❑ Gotten all necessary prescriptions for the trip filled
- ❑ Called and confirmed your air reservations at least 72 hours in advance
- ❑ Verified with all airlines current luggage weight limits and number of pieces allowed
- ❑ Spoken to the house sitter about duties
- ❑ Arranged for mail/paper holds while away
- ❑ Filled in your Trip Expense Summary
- ❑ Finalized Reservations Summary pages and distributed them to your support team
- ❑ Confirmed all information on your Support "A Team" Contact List
- ❑ Completed everything on The Day Before I Leave checklist

You will find three forms in this section that I encourage you to use to track all the logistics for your upcoming trip. The forms, as appropriate, can be carried with you, scanned into your PDA or phone, emailed to yourself, and left with your support team, neighbors, and supervisor at your job as appropriate.

17. Trip Expense Summary

Volunteer Agency		Subtotal
Deposit	$ _____	
Final Payment	$ _____	_____
Flights		
International	$ _____	
Within Country	$ _____	_____
Other Transportation	$ _____	_____
Hotels		
First Night	$ _____	
Last Night	$ _____	_____
Food	$ _____	_____
Passport	$ _____	_____
Visas	$ _____	_____
Vaccinations	$ _____	
Medications	$ _____	
Medical Insurance	$ _____	_____
Trip Insurance	$ _____	_____
Special Equipment	$ _____	_____
Potential TAX DEDUCT TOTAL		_____
Vacation Hotel	$ _____	_____
Transportation	$ _____	_____
Food	$ _____	_____
Excursions	$ _____	_____
Other Expenses	$ _____	_____
VACATION SUBTOTAL		_____
TRIP TOTAL		_____

18. Reservations Summary

(Make copies for you and your house sitter, relatives, work contacts.)

Volunteer Agency _____

Website _____ Address _____

U.S. Contact _____ Phone _____ Email _____

In-Country Contact _____ Phone _____ Email _____

Flights

Booking Engine/Agent   Airline   Phone   Email

_____

Confirmation Code _____ Amount _____

Date	Airline	Flight #	City	Departs	Arrives	City

Other Transportation

Agency   Phone   Email   Website

_____

Confirmation Code _____ Amount _____

Date	Transportation	Res #	City	Departs	Arrives	City

Hotels or Other Lodging

Booking Agent _____   Phone _____   Email _____

Hotels _____   Phone _____

Address _____   Website _____

Email _____

Date	Hotel	Confirm #	City	Arrives	Departs	Rate/Night

Tours

Tour _____   Phone _____

Address _____   Website _____

Email _____

Date	Tour	City	Confirm #	Departs	Return	Amount

19. Support "A Team" Contact List

	Name	Phone	Email
Accountant/Bookkeeper			
Dentist			
Doctor			
Family Members			
Health Insurance			
Home/Car Insurance			
House sitter			
Lawyer			
Medical Power of Attorney			
Pet Sitter			
Power of Attorney			
Tax Advisor			
Travel Agent			
Trip Insurance			
Veterinarian			
Volunteer Agency			

20 The Day Before I Leave Checklist

❏ Deliver animals to pet sitter or boarding facility

❏ Re-confirm tomorrow's flights, especially international legs

❏ Print out boarding passes if possible

❏ Finalize packing and weigh my luggage

❏ Confirm pickup time for my ride to the airport

❏ Call and confirm pickup person and date for return ride from the airport

❏ Breathe deeply and often

❏ Plan to get a good night's sleep

Final Advice

Arrive early to the airport for check-in, then sit back and enjoy the start of your volunteer vacation!

Part Six: Special Trips

After Part Six, you will have:

- ❑ Read Chapters 21 to 23
- ❑ If appropriate, begun mapping logistics for your extended trip
- ❑ If appropriate, divided up the duties for a family/group trip
- ❑ Gained ideas for planning your volunteer vacation *without* using a placement agency

Extended Trips

If you will be away for more than four weeks or an even longer amount of time, several of the earlier sections in this book may take on new meaning, particularly developing your "A Team."

Developing Your "A Team"

You will want to gather a strong "A Team" of the people who will look after things at home and manage your affairs while you are away. Once you have your "A Team" in place, sit down with the team members and discuss their assignments. If you have multiple people on your team, make sure they know whom to contact for certain issues.

Create a sheet with each person's contact information and what they will handle on your behalf. Distribute copies to the entire team. Have both an electronic or emailed and paper copy with you so you can easily access information.

My "A Team"

When I left for my year away, I had not located a tenant for my townhome. My three cats were still in residence, and my cat sitter came twice daily to care for them. My pets were okay the first month, not so great the second month, and downright unhappy the third month. After a conference call among my rental agent, pet sitter, Power of Attorney, and main contact person, they decided to have my cats live with the pet sitter for the remainder of the year and rent out my townhome. At the time, I had no guarantee my cats would get along with the pet sitter's animals. Thanks to my "A Team," I am happy to report, all worked out incredibly well. The townhome was rented, my cats got along well with others, and they were happy to come home to me when I returned. What would I have been able to do long distance if I hadn't had my "A Team" in place?

Long-Term Considerations

Before you leave for an extended time, consider each of these areas and the best resolution for you:

Job – sabbatical, terminate job, or retire?

Home – sell, sublet, or rent?

Possessions – Sell, store, donate, or give them away?

Car or other large piece of equipment – Sell, lend, donate, or store it?

Are You Covered?

If you will be out of the country for more than six months, some health insurance companies may not cover you while you're away or when you return. It's best to know this in advance and determine the best solution for you and your situation.

Insurance – What does your house, car, belongings, trip, or health insurance cover while you are on the road—and after you return?

Will, Durable Power of Attorney (POA), Medical POA – These documents need to be in place.

Pets/Plants – sitter, relative, or permanent new home?

Mail, taxes, elections, and investment obligations – If these items are time sensitive, what is your backup plan if you can't find Internet or phone coverage? Who has authority to make decisions for you? Who will take care of your mail and/or handle anything that comes up or notify you for direction? If you want to mail things home while you are away, who will accept and store them for you?

Commitments to others – If you have power of attorney (POA) for someone else or are an executor of a will, who will step in for you if you're not available? How will you handle graduations, births, weddings, anniversaries, or deaths? Under what circumstances might you come home for a brief time, or cancel the remainder of the trip and come home permanently?

Planning an extensive trip requires considerable effort to get all the logistics settled. Allow plenty of time to make the best decisions for yourself, not only when you are away, but for when you return.

Notes

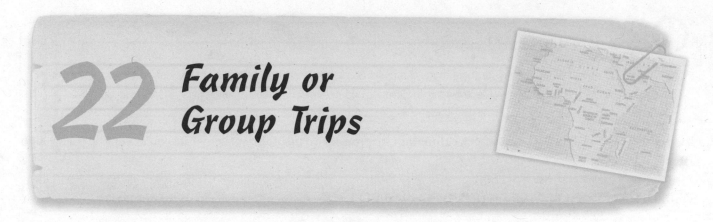

22 Family or Group Trips

How exciting it will be to share your volunteer trip with like-minded family members and/or friends!

Spreading the Responsibility

With careful planning and direct discussions, you can share the responsibility and multiply the fun. You might—

Divide and Delegate – Usually one person in a group is considered the trip-flight organizer/map reader/meal locator/activity planner. While this person may be able to do it all, s/he will likely appreciate sharing some responsibilities with others. I suggest getting your travel group together (in person, on the phone, or electronically), and assign duties for each person to research. Have them bring their research to the next meeting to discuss and decide who will handle what.

Share Suitcases – For two people traveling together, try suitcase sharing. First, pile the clothes you plan to take in one area. Take half your clothes to the other person's suitcase and pack them, and then have that person do the same. Then pack your remaining clothes in your own suitcase. This way, if one suitcase is delayed, you both have clothes to wear until the errant suitcase is recovered.

Plan for Time to Yourself – Just remember this famous quotation by **Benjamin Franklin** in *Poor Richard's Almanac* in 1736: *"Fish and visitors stink in three days."*

While this may not sound like an appropriate quotation about traveling, it may apply. Yes, you love your family and friends. Just remember that traveling together can be confining at times. Discuss with your fellow travelers before you depart what kind of time and how much of it will be spent as a group and how much time will be spent alone. You might get so wrapped up in the trip and the adventures that you never need alone time. If you find you want to be alone, however, you will be pleased you negotiated it beforehand to avoid hurting anyone's feelings during the trip.

Carry Only One of Each

While traveling in Thailand, I met four American women who get together every other year and volunteer with Earthwatch on an archaeological dig. Because they live in three different cities, they do all the planning by email and phone calls. After they'd completed two trips together, they coordinated who brought what for the group to share for the third trip. On our trip, between them they had every medical supply and piece of equipment needed, with backups for emergencies. The quartet even purchased a communal trip cell phone with a SIM card. For future trips, they will simply buy a SIM card for the new country, load it with minutes, and then they will be ready to go. Way to coordinate!

Missing the Familiar

"I just want to do something like at HOME!" No matter how thrilling the trip, some people in your group may need recognizable things and experiences like those at home to tame the adrenaline rush or just feel comfortable. It is not a sin to occasionally find a coffee bar and lounge for a few hours, get lost in a western-style shopping mall, take in a movie in English, or even patronize a McDonald's or Starbucks. Sometimes that little dose of so-called luxury (or normalcy) gives over-stimulated travelers time to balance, regroup, and gain perspective so they can continue to enjoy the exotic nature of the trip. Actually, visiting a McDonald's in another country can be a hoot, if only to see what's different on the menu than what you'd find at home. By the way, if you are looking for dependable wireless Internet connections, McDonald's and Starbucks overseas tend to have WiFi.

Notes

23 A Trip Without a a Volunteer Placement Agency

Finding and planning a volunteer vacation through a placement agency offers a package experience with most of the details finalized. However, some volunteers prefer to do all the research, planning, organizing, and facilitating themselves. Not using a volunteer placement agency can add adventure to the trip, while allowing your travel plans to remain flexible. It may also be possible to save money.

Doing It Yourself

When you do it yourself, all logistics, research, and plans are your responsibility. This includes airfare, local transportation, work location, lodging and food, insurance, and finding organizations that need your assistance. Some volunteer travelers opt to purchase an airline ticket to a foreign locale and then, once they land, decide what to do, whom to work with, and when to start. If asking around does not locate the right fit for you, you can go to Idealist at **www.idealist.org** to research possible options.

 Choice of Project

Keep in mind that some volunteer projects are only accessible through a volunteer placement agency, so you may be limited in your choices when you go solo.

The Minimum of Arrangements

When finding your own volunteer work, your research may include:

- Which local NGOs need volunteers

- What work you will do

- Where you will stay. There is usually a fee for your room and board to the local agency. Sometimes, an organization that needs volunteers will house you either in a dormitory or at a home stay in exchange for your work efforts.

- When/where you will eat

- How you will get back and forth from your volunteer work

Organizations That May Offer You Increased Flexibility

Some organizations offer volunteers some flexibility over what and when to work, with whom, and length of stay. They include:

- Green Volunteers – **www.greenvolunteers.org**
- WWOOF – World Wide Opportunities On Organic Farms – **www.wwoof.org**
- Churches, NGOs, or social service agencies
- Mother Teresa's Hospital in Calcutta – See Resources

Doing It Yourself

Although planning your volunteer vacation yourself may provide lower costs and greater flexibility than working through an agency, it may not offer you consistency of experience, insurance, support while in the country, and tax deductibility when you return home.

Many organizations do not have the financial resources for extensive advertising and depend on foreign volunteers to help with their work. By researching carefully and corresponding in advance with the organization in the foreign country before you arrive, and speaking to previous volunteers if at all possible, you should be able to find worthy organizations on your own and make satisfactory arrangements.

Notes

Part Seven: Resources

In Part Seven, you will find chapters with website links and print resources for:

- ❑ Volunteer Agencies I Used
- ❑ Additional Volunteer Agencies and Websites
- ❑ Travel-Related Websites
- ❑ Reading Suggestions
- ❑ Glossary
- ❑ Time Zones Map

Note: These lists by no means reflect a complete listing of every agency, book, magazine, or ezine devoted to volunteer vacations or international travel. Rather, consider them a starting point for planning your own volunteer vacation adventure.

24 Volunteer Agencies I Used

* Indicates a U.S. nonprofit (The specific projects are in parenthesis.)

AACE Inc. – info@aace.org.au

P.O. Box 47, Marlborough QLD 4705, Australia

www.aace.org.au (Wallaby project near Rockhampton, Australia)

CARE – care@lantic.net

P.O. Box 1937, Phalaborwa 1390, South Africa

www.primatecare.org.za (Baboon sanctuary near Kruger Park in South Africa)

Eagle's Nest Wildlife Hospital – info@wildlife-sanctuary.info

P.O. Box 282, Ravenshoe QLD 4888, Australia

www.wildlife-sanctuary.info (Wildlife hospital near Cairns, Australia)

Earthwatch * – info@earthwatch.org, 800-776-0188

3 Clocktower Place, Suite 100, Box 75, Maynard MA 01754-0075

www.earthwatch.org (Scientific projects; archaeology in Thailand and koalas and echidnas in Australia)

Enkosini – info@enkosini.com, 206-604-2664

506 Overlake Drive E., Medina WA 98039

www.enkosiniecoexperience.com (Umbrella organization for South African Wildlife)

Global Volunteers * – email@globalvolunteers.org, 800-487-1074

375 E. Little Canada Rd., St. Paul MN 55117-1628

www.globalvolunteers.org (Children's issues – Orphans in Peru and Romania and English tutoring and Red Cross work in the Cook Islands)

I-to-I – info@i-to-i.com, 800-985-4864

Woodside House, 261 Low Ln., Horsforth, Leeds, LS185NY United Kingdom

www.i-to-i.com (Placements at AACE, Eagle's Nest and Lion Park in South Africa)

Pueblo Ingles – info@puebloingles.com, (1 34) 913-913-400

Rafael Calvo 18, 4A, Madrid 28010, Spain

www.vaughanvillage.com (English conversation intensive program)

La Sabranenque – info@sabranenque.com

La Sabranenque, rue de la Tour de l'Oume, 30290 St. Victor la Coste, France

www.sabranenque.com (Medieval reconstruction near Avignon, France)

SANCCOB – info@sanccob.co.za

P.O. Box 11116, Bloubergrant Cape Town 7443, South Africa

www.sanccob.co.za (South African Penguin hospital - Cape Town, S. Africa)

25 Additional Volunteer Agency Websites

Note: This is only a *small sample* of possible volunteer agencies.

To Find Local, Domestic, and International Opportunities

Charity Guide – **www.charityguide.org**

Idealist – **www.idealist.org**

Volunteer Match – **www.volunteermatch.org**

Volunteer Organizations – **www.volunteerinternational.org**

Volunteer Solutions – **www.volunteersolutions.org**

Other Volunteer Websites to Consider

American Jewish World Service – **www.ajws.org**

American Trails – **www.americantrail.org**

AmeriCorps – **www.americorps.gov**

Amerispan Unlimited – **www.amerispan.com**

Airline Ambassadors – **www.airlineamb.org**

Amizade – **www.amizade.org**

AVIVA – **www.aviva-sa.org/en/**

Biosphere, North America – **www.biosphere-expeditions.org**

Catholic Network of Volunteer Service – **www.cnvs.org**

Cross Cultural Solutions – **www.crossculturalsolutions.org**

Doctors without Borders – **www.doctorswithoutborders.org**

Dragonfly – **www.thai-dragonfly.com**

Elderhostel – **www.elderhostel.org**

Experiential Learning International – **www.eliabroad.org**

Family Opportunities – **www.doinggoodtogether.org**

Food for the Hungry – **www.fh.org**

Global Children's Network – **www.globalchild.org**

Global Citizens Network – **www.globalcitizens.org**

Global Routes – **www.globalroutes.org**

Global Service Corps – **www.globalservicecorps.org**

Global Vision International – **www.gvi.co.uk**

Global Volunteer Network – **www.volunteer.org.nz**

Go Abroad – **www.goabroad.com**

Greenpeace – **www.greenpeace.org**

Habitat for Humanity – **www.habitat.org**

Heifer International – **www.heifer.org**

Heritage Conservation – **www.heritageconservation.net**

Institute of Field Research Expeditions – **www.ifrevolunteers.org**

Inter Action – **www.interaction.org**

Interactive Voluntary Development Network – Kenya – **www.ivdn-africa.org**

International Executive Service Corps – **www.isec.org**

Iona Community and Abbey – **www.iona.org.uk**

Islamic Relief USA – **www.irw.org**

Kenyan Children Foundation – **www.kenyanchildrenfoundation.org**

Mother Teresa's Hospital – 54a Lower Circular Rd., Kolkata 700016, West Bengal, India

Namaste India Children's Fund – **www.nicfund.org**

National Retiree Volunteer Coalition – **www.voa.org**

Oceanic Society Expeditions – **www.oceanic-society.org/**

Peace Corps – **www.peacecorps.gov**

Physicians for Peace – **www.physiciansforpeace.org**

Points of Light Foundation – **www.pointsoflight.org**

Project HOPE – **www.projecthope.org**

Prosthetics Outreach Foundation – **www.pofsea.org**

REI Adventures – **www.rei.com/aboutrei/volunteer.html**

Save the Children – **www.savethechildren.org**

Sierra Club – **www.sierraclub.org**

Sports for at risk youth – **www.joyofsports.org**

Student Conservation Association – **www.thesca.org**

Teach Abroad – **www.teachabroad.com**

USA Freedom Corps Volunteer Network – **www.usafreedomcorps.gov**

United Nations Volunteers – **www.unv.org**

Volunteer Adventures – **www.volunteeradventures.com**

Volunteer for the Government – **www.volunteer.gov/gov**

Volunteers for Peace – **www.vfp.org**

Volunteer Service Overseas – **www.vso.org.uk**

World Teach – **www.worldteach.org**

World Wide Volunteer – **www.worldwidevolunteer.org**

26 Travel-Related Websites

(** Indicates organizations I have used)

Airlines

American Airlines – **www.aa.com**

Continental Airlines – **www.flycontinental.com**

Delta Airlines – **www.delta.com**

United Airlines – **www.united.com**

Airline Search Engines

Airfarewatchdog – **www.airfarewatchdog.com**

Expedia – **www.expedia.com**

Kayak – **www.kayak.com**

Orbitz – **www.orbitz.com**

Priceline – **www.priceline.com**

Sidestep – **www.sidestep.com**

Travelocity – **www.travelocity.com**

Around-the-World Air Tickets

Air Brokers – **www.airbrokers.com**

AirTreks ** – **www.airtreks.com**

Bootsnall – **www.bootsnall.com**

STAtravel (says students only, but also for teachers and educators) – **www.statravel.com**

Travel Blogs

TravBuddy – **www.travbuddy.com**

Travel Blog – **www.travelblog.com**

Travellerspoint ** – **www.travellerspoint.com**

Business Cards

Vista Print ** – **www.vistaprint.com**

Customs/Immigration

U.S. Customs ** – **www.cbp.gov/xp/cgov/travel**

Australia ** – **www.immi.gov.au**

Green Travel Issues

Carbon Fund – **www.carbonfund.org**

Ethical Traveler – **www.ethicaltraveler.org**

Native Energy – **www.nativeenergy.com**

Responsible Travel – **www.responsibletravel.com**

Sustainable Travel – **www.sustainabletravel.com**

Terra Pass ** – **www.terrapass.com**

Health Issues/Immunizations

Centers for Disease Control ** – **www.cdc.gov**

World Health Organization – **www.who.int**

Hotels/Hostels/Accommodations

Asiarooms ** - **www.asiarooms.com**

Couch Surfing – **www.couchsurfing.com**

Europe Hostels – **www.europehostels.com**

Hostelling International ** – **www.hihostels.com**

Hostels – **www.hostels.com**

Ibis Hotels – **www.ibishotel.com**

Monastery Stays – **www.monasterystays.com**

Novotel – **www.novotel.com**

House Sitting/House Swap

Digsville – **www.digsville.com**

Home Exchange – **www.homeexchange.com**

Home Link – **www.homelink.org**

House Carers – www.housecarers.com

Mind My House – www.mindmyhouse.com

Sabbatical Homes – www.sabbaticalhomes.com

Insurance - Travel - Trip delay, Luggage, Medical

Travelex – www.travelex-insurance.com

AIG Travel Guard – www.travelguard.com

World Nomads – www.worldnomads.com

Tripplus – www.tripplus.com (students only)

Insurance - Travel - Technology

Safeware – www.safeware.com

Insurance - Travel - Medical Evacuation

Medjet Assist – www.medjetassist.com

Global Rescue – www.globalrescue.com

Internet/Phone Service

Global Gossip ** – www.globalgossip.com

PostNet ** – www.postnet.com

Skype ** – www.skype.com

Luggage

Changes in Latitude ** – www.cil.com

Eagle Creek ** – www.eaglecreek.com

EMS – www.ems.com

REI ** – www.rei.com

Samsonite ** – www.samsonite.com

Tumi ** – www.tumi.com

Mail and Freight

DHL – www.dhl.com

FedEx ** – www.fedex.com

Global Gossip ** – www.globalgossip.com

Postnet ** – www.postnet.com

U.S. Postal Service – www.usps.com

Meeting the Locals

Coach surfing – www.couchsurfing.com

Journey Woman ** – www.journeywoman.com

Servas – www.servas.org

Money Exchange Rates

XE ** – www.xe.com/ucc

X-Rates – www.x-rates.com

Passports and Visas

U.S. Passport ** – www.travel.state.gov/passport

U.S. Postal Service ** – www.usps.com

Visa Agencies – www.traveldocs.com

www.visahq.com

www.urgentpassport.com

Australian Electronic Visa ** – www.immi.gov.au

Photo Sharing

Flickr – www.flickr.com

Fotki – www.fotki.com

Pbase – www.pbase.com

Shutterfly – www.shutterfly.com

Smugmug – www.smugmug.com

Snappages – www.snappages.com

Rail Tickets – Europe

Bootsnall – www.bootsnall.com

Britrail ** – www.britrail.com

Eurail ** – www.eurail.com

Rick Steves ** – www.ricksteves.com

Sales Tax Refunds

General Information – www.traveltax.msu.edu/vat/vat.htm

General Information – www.foxnomad.com/2008/03/
06/how-to-reclaim-taxes-paid-abroad

General Information for Europe –
www.europeforvisitors.com

Australia – www.customs.gov.au/site/page.cfm?u=5347

Travel Agencies/Clubs/Tours

AAA – www.aaa.com

AirTreks – www.airtreks.com

American Express – www.americanexpress.com

Rick Steves – www.ricksteves.com

USAA (U.S. Military only) – www.usaa.com

Travel Registration with the U.S. State Department

State Department – https://travelregistration.state.gov/

U.S. Travel Security

TSA – www.tsa.gov

Vacation Destinations

UNESCO Sites ** – http://whc.unesco.org/

27 Reading Suggestions

Books on Volunteering or International Travel

Adventures of a Continental Drifter: An Around-the World Excursion into Weirdness, Danger, Lust and the Perils of Street Food. Elliot Hester. New York: St. Martins Press, 2005.

The Art of Pilgrimage; The Seekers Guide to Making Travel Sacred. Phil Cosineau. California: Conari Press, 1998.

The Busy Family's Guide to Volunteering: Do Good, Have Fun, Make a Difference as a Family! Jenny Friedman. Maryland: Robins Lane, 2003.

Chicken Soup for the Traveler's Soul – Jack Canfield, et al. Deerfield Beach: Health Communications, 2002.

Code Green: Experiences of a Lifetime. Lonely Planet Publications, 2006.

Green Volunteers: The World Guide to Voluntary Work in Nature Conservation – 6th Edition. Italy: We Care Guides – Green Volunteers, 2007.

How to Live Your Dreams of Volunteering Overseas. Joseph Collins, et al. New York: Penguin, 2002.

The Hundred Best Vacations to Enrich Your Life. Pam Grout. Washington, D.C.: National Geographic, 2008.

International Directory of Voluntary Work – 9th Edition. Victoria Pybus. United Kingdom, 2005

The Road Within: True Stories of Transformation. Sean, James and Tim O'Reilly, Editors. San Francisco: Travelers' Tales, 2002.

Teaching English Abroad, 8th Edition. Susan Griffith. United Kingdom: VacationWork, 2007

Volunteer: A Traveler's Guide to Making a Difference Around the World. Lonely Planet Publications, 2007

Volunteer Vacations – 8th Edition. Bill McMillan, et al. Chicago: Chicago Review Press, 2003

Volunteering Around the Globe. Suzanne Stone. Sterling: Capitol Books, 2008.

Volunteering the Selfish Benefit: Achieve Deep-Down Satisfaction and Create that Desire in Others. Charles A. Bennett. Oak View: Committee Communications, 2001.

The Way of the Traveler: Making Every Trip a Journey of Self-Discovery – 2nd Edition. Joseph Dispenza. California: Avalon Travel, 2002.

Work Your Way Around the World – 11th Edition. Susan Griffith. United Kingdom: Vacation Work, 2004.

World Abroad: Complete Guide to Finding a Job Overseas – 4th Edition. Clayton Hubbs, Editor. Transitions Abroad Publishing, 2002.

Guidebooks

Your Heart's Desire: *Instructions for Creating the Life You Really Want.* Sonia Choquette. New York: Three Rivers Press, 1997.

Gutsy Women: More Travel Tips and Wisdom for the Road – 2nd Edition. Marybeth Bond. San Francisco: Travelers' Tales, 2001.

Kiss, Bow or Shake Hands: *How to Do Business in Sixty Countries.* Terri Morrison, et al. Avon: Adams Media, 1994.

Lonely Planet – City and Country Guides. Lonely Planet Publications, updated annually.

Rick Steves' Europe and Country Guides. Rick Steves. Emeryville: Avalon Travel, updated annually.

Preparing To Return Home

The Absentee American: Repatriates' Perspectives on America. Carolyn D. Smith. Bayside: Aletheia, 1994

Magazines and Online Ezines

Arthur Frommer's Budget Travel – **www.budgettravel.com**

InsideOut Web Magazine – **www.insideoutmag.com**

International Travel News – **www.intltravelnews.com**

Journey Women – **www.journeywoman.com**

National Geographic Traveler or Adventure – **www.nationalgeographic.com**

Student Traveler – **www.studenttraveler.com**

Transitions Abroad – **www.transitionsabroad.com**

Verge – Travel on Purpose – **www.vergemagazine.ca**

28 Glossary

Consulate – A consul's office or official residence. There can be multiple consuls and consulates in any country. Consulates take care of many of the same administrative duties as embassies.

Embassy – The residence and place of business of an ambassador. There is only one embassy for each foreign country and it is traditionally in the capital city of the host country. Embassies take care of the same administrative duties as consulates, but they also represent their governments abroad.

En-Suite – A lodging that has a private bathroom attached. This can sometimes mean only the toilet is attached or it could also mean the room has a shower or tub as well.

Nonprofit Organization – Organizations that are designated under the U.S. IRS code as not-for-profit, and the website usually has the ending "dot-org".

NGO – Non-Governmental Agency – Same as a U.S. Nonprofit Organization in countries other than the U.S. and their website also usually ends in "dot-org".

Oceania – (Sometimes Oceanica) According to Wikipedia, this is a geographical, often geopolitical, region consisting of numerous lands—mostly islands in the Pacific Ocean and vicinity. Ethnologically, the islands that are included in Oceania are divided into the sub regions of Melanesia, Micronesia, and Polynesia.

> **Melanesia** is a sub region of Oceania extending from the western side of the West Pacific to the Arafura Sea, north and northeast of Australia. The term was first used to denote an ethnic and geographical grouping of islands south of the equator that are distinct from Polynesia and Micronesia. There is a widely used geopolitical conception of the term Melanesia, which is comprised of the islands or nations of Vanuatu, Solomon Islands, Papua New Guinea, and Fiji.

> **Micronesia** is a sub region of Oceania, comprising hundreds of small islands in the Pacific Ocean. The islands are predominantly above the equator with the Philippines to the northwest, Indonesia, Papua New Guinea, and Melanesia to the west and south, and Polynesia to the east. This region is made up of the island nations of Guam, Kiribati, Marshall Islands, Federated States of Micronesia (FSM), Nauru, Northern Mariana Islands, Palau, and Wake Island.

> **Polynesia** is generally defined as the islands within the Polynesian triangle. The term "Polynesia," meaning many islands, was first used to describe all the islands of the Pacific. Geographically, Polynesia may be described as the islands that fall within a triangle with its corners at Hawaii, New Zealand, and Easter Island.

Passport – An official document issued by the government of a country to a citizen that identifies the bearer and gives permission to travel to and from that country

Placement – A volunteer or work assignment through an agency

Power of Attorney (POA) –

> **Medical Power of Attorney** – The legal authority to act for another person on medical matters

> **Power of Attorney or Durable Power of Attorney** – The legal authority to act for another person in legal and business matters

Self-Catering – On a volunteer placement, this usually mean you have to do your own cooking or share the cooking responsibilities. Sometimes food is provided; other times, you must also shop for the food as well.

Travel Insurance Terms –

> **Emergency Medical** – Generally, medical coverage over and above your U.S. health insurance coverage for any illness, accident, medication, or hospitalization that occurs while you are out of the country.

> **Medical Evacuation** – If necessary, air transportation to the closest hospital. This can mean to the closest hospital that offers Western healthcare or the closest hospital in the country. Check with the individual policy for the exact specifications.

> **Repatriation** – Covers the return to the U.S. of the body or remains if there is a death overseas

> **Trip Cancellation** – Reimburses you for prepaid, nonrefundable expenses, such as airline tickets, if you are forced to cancel a trip due to an unforeseen emergency.

> **Trip Delay or Interruption** – If you are delayed for more than a stipulated number of hours such as common carrier delays; traffic accidents; weather conditions; lost or stolen money or travel documents; natural disasters; terrorism; etc., you will be paid the benefits provided by your policy. These benefits may include money to help you to return home or rejoin your trip. They may also include compensation for any unused and nonrefundable portion of your trip.

> **Airline Default** – Not usually a named, stand-alone policy, this can be included within Trip Delay or Interruption coverage. This coverage would compensate you if the airline you were using defaults or stops flying. Ask your insurance agent if the policy you are considering covers Airline Default.

Visa – An official endorsement in a passport authorizing the bearer to enter or leave, and travel in or through, a particular country or region; any mark of official authorization

Will, as in Last Will and Testament – A legal document that gives your wishes for the disposal of your assets and property upon your death

Whoop Whoop – (Australia) Outback, miles from anywhere

29. Time Zones Map

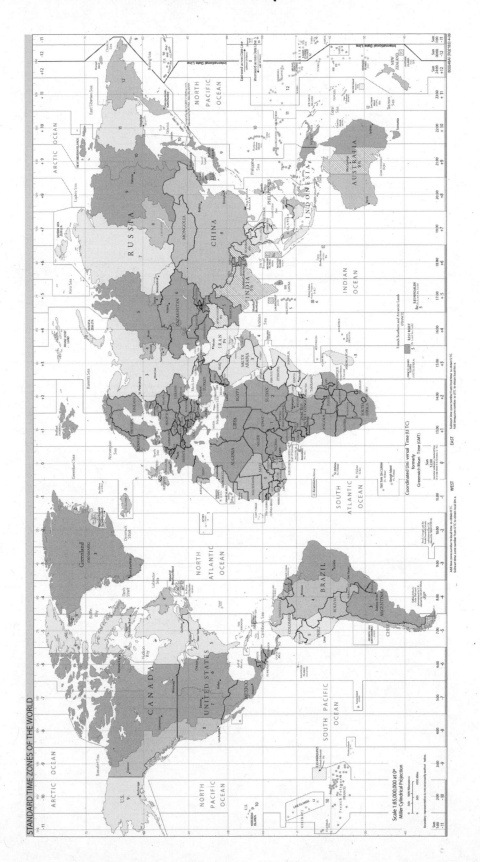

Afterword

As a volunteer and international traveler, I know how much fun it is to meet new people while you volunteer and vacation with like-minded travelers. Once bitten, you want to do it all the time.

Something inside you will make an incredible difference to the agencies or causes that you honor with your support of time and money. It will also make a difference to your fellow volunteers.

I do not want you to end your reading thinking, "This book sure covers everything you need to know before you go" or saying, "Wow, Jane really is an organizer." Instead, I want you to resolve to get out there yourself and share your talents with the world.

I look forward to meeting you and hope to do so at a volunteer placement in the near future.

Travel in Safety,

Jane Stanfield
Where Is She Heading
www.janestanfieldwish.com

About the Author

Jane Stanfield combined her master's of science degree in animal science with her immense love of travel and a passion for volunteering during a yearlong volunteer vacation.

In Colorado since 1983, Jane has worked in non-profit and governmental sectors for more than 20 years as an administrator and program coordinator. Active as a volunteer on projects such as therapeutic horseback riding, recording for the blind, and part-time actress/choreographer in community theatre, Jane expanded her horizons with the yearlong trip in 2006.

A class titled "Your Heart's Desire" based on the book by Sonia Choquette and led by Peter J. Hughes (**www.peterjhughes.com**) was the catalyst. Jane read everything available on the topic of volunteer vacations so she could map out her own volunteer adventure. Part way through her planning, Jane received an inheritance that made her trip possible.

Originally, Jane planned a trip of three to four months, but more research persuaded her to take an entire year to explore, volunteer, and vacation. Her goal? To return with a larger worldview and a stronger idea where to focus her energy.

With a stuffed penguin as company, Jane visited 11 countries in six continents, and completed 12 volunteer placements over 12 months. Three pairs of shoes, three pieces of luggage, lots of zip-lock bags for packing, and a Lonely Planet Book for each country went along. She especially enjoyed her vacations at UNESCO World Heritage Sites, including Easter Island and Angkor Wat.

Today, through her company Where Is She Heading, Jane gives presentations, offers workshops, and provides individual coaching for people planning volunteer vacations. She teaches "Volunteer Vacations, Traveling on Purpose" at the Colorado Free University (**www.freeu.com**) and coordinates the Travel Lovers' Book Club at the Tattered Cover Bookstore (either at **www.janestanfieldwish.com** or **www.tatteredcover.com**).

In addition to her articles and tips about volunteer vacation travel, she's planning to release other books in 2009 about her yearlong trip.

Jane lives in Lakewood, Colorado, with her two cats Worry Wart and Moonbeam. For more information on Where Is She Heading, visit her website at **www.janestanfieldwish.com**.

Here's where she headed in 2006 (volunteer placements in bold):

Month	Name of Agency	Country	Purpose
Jan	**Global Volunteers**	**Peru**	**Working with orphans**
	Machu Picchu		Vacation
	Various locations		Vacation
	Dance Camp		Vacation
Feb	Easter Island	Chile	Vacation
	Earthwatch	**Thailand**	**Archaeology – Origins of Angkor**
Mar	Angkor Wat	Cambodia	Vacation
	Various locations	Thailand	Vacation
	Global Volunteers	**Cook Islands**	**Teaching English, Red Cross work**
Apr	Various locations	New Zealand	Vacation
May	**Earthwatch**	**Australia**	**Koala Ecology**
	Airle Beach	Australia	Vacation - Barrier Reef
Jun	**I to I**	**Australia**	**AACE - Wallaby Rehabilitation**
	Adelaide	Australia	Vacation
Jul	**Earthwatch**	**Australia**	**Echidnas and Goannas**
	Sydney/Cairns	Australia	Vacation
Aug	**I to I**	**Australia**	**Eagle's Nest Wildlife Hospital**
	Hong Kong	Hong Kong	Vacation
Sep	**Enkosini**	**South Africa**	**CARE – Baboon sanctuary**
Oct	**Enkosini**	**South Africa**	**SANCCOB – Penguin hospital**
Nov	**I to I**	**South Africa**	**Lion Park**
	Pueblo Ingles	**Spain**	**English language intensive**
Dec	**Global Volunteers**	**Romania**	**Working with Orphans**
	London	England	Vacation

Mapping Your Volunteer Vacation Workbook
U.S. **$20.00**
CAN **$25.00**

Mapping Your Volunteer Vacation on CD
U.S. **$15.00**
CAN **$20.00**

Ask about quantity discounts when you order 5 or more products.

SALES TAX - Please add 7.6% sales tax per book or CD for products shipped to a Colorado address.

U.S. SHIPPING - $5.00 for the first book or CD and add $1.50 for each additional product.

INT'L. SHIPPING - $10.00 for the first book or CD and add $5.00 for each additional product.

Ask about lower shipping rates for quantities of books over 5.

Ask about having Jane speak at your conference or meeting.

Thank you for your order.

JANE STANFIELD
WHERE IS SHE HEADING
P.O. BOX 27482
LAKEWOOD, CO 80227

ORDER FORM

TELEPHONE ORDERS - 303-988-1356

Ordered by:

Name

Title _____ Date

Company

Address

City _____ State _____ Zip

Online orders and credit card payments can be made at www.janestanfieldwish.com

Items ordered:

Item #	Description	Cost Each	Quantity	Item Total

SALES TAX - Please add 7.6% sales tax per book or CD for products shipped to a Colorado address.

Total price of items	
Tax (if applicable)	
Add shipping charge	
Total Amount Enclosed	

Methods of payment:

Please charge my: ☐ Discover   ☐ MasterCard   ☐ VISA   ☐ AMEX Card

Number: ☐☐☐☐☐☐☐☐☐☐☐☐☐☐☐☐ Expiration Date

(Month/Year): ☐☐ / ☐☐

Signature (as shown on credit card): _____

Check or Money Order

Check # _____   Total Payment $_____

Please make checks payable to **Jane Stanfield**.

Postal orders with checks:

Where Is She Heading, P.O. Box 27482, Lakewood, CO 80227

Charting Your Course

A Volunteer's Wish List

Ever wonder what it feels like to …

- Bottle-feed an infant baboon?
- Sing a lullaby to a Peruvian orphan?
- See a grade-school dance performance in another country?
- Teach art to the most appreciative kids you have ever seen?
- Build a house for a wonderful family living in a shanty?
- Gently lift a 3000-year-old Neolithic pot from its carefully excavated dirt?
- Play soccer with children in a developing nation and get your butt kicked?

A volunteer vacation lets you experience similar wonders and many more.

Myriad of Options

The Charting Your Course foldout offers you a beginning list of the thousands of combinations of volunteer opportunities. From the possibilities you discover on the chart, you can eventually pinpoint a project that fits your schedule, budget, and volunteer goals—as well as your heart.

Yes, I understand that all these options can send your mind spinning. But the only question you have to answer right now is this:

What do you want to do FIRST?

With that question in mind, turn the page, open this Chart, and begin to map the most fabulous volunteer vacation ever. It's your turn to dream!

Your Turn to Dream!

As I said, your choices can appear overwhelming. Before you proceed to answer the "what to do first" question, I invite you to spend time dreaming about your volunteer trip, focusing on your desires and other details.

Examples: I want to work with elephants anywhere they occur. (what)

I want to do something in Australia. (where)

I want to volunteer in Peru so I can visit Machu Picchu (where and what)

Your Turn

I want to work with _____ in _____. (what, where)

I want to work with _____ in _____. (what, where)

I want to be in _____ in _____to see _____. (where, when, what)

I want to be in _____ in _____to see _____. (where, when, what)

I want to see _____ in _____. (what, where)

I want to see _____ in _____. (what, where)

I want to go to _____ in _____. (where, when)

I want to go to _____ in _____. (where, when)

I want to work for _____ in _____. (who, where)

I want to work for _____ in _____. (who, where)

I want to vacation in _____. (where)

I want to vacation in _____. (where)

BUSINESS REPLY MAIL

JANE STANFIELD
WHERE IS SHE HEADING
P.O. BOX 27482
LAKEWOOD, CO 80227

BUSINESS REPLY MAIL

JANE STANFIELD
WHERE IS SHE HEADING
P.O. BOX 27482
LAKEWOOD, CO 80227

Where Is She Heading

Please Tell Us...

What did you do on your last volunteer vacation? What tips can you offer a prospective volunteer? What insights can you share for future editions of the book, or "tips and ideas" email newsletter? Please write your ideas below, then stamp and mail the postcard or email me thoughts at **mapppingyvv@me.com**.

_____

_____

_____

_____

Check here: __ Yes, please share my idea.   __ Yes, you can use my name.

                 __ Yes, please email me the free quarterly "tips and ideas" newsletter

Name: _____

Email: _____

Where Is She Heading

Please Tell Us...

What did you do on your last volunteer vacation? What tips can you offer a prospective volunteer? What insights can you share for future editions of the book, or "tips and ideas" email newsletter? Please write your ideas below, then stamp and mail the postcard or email me thoughts at **mapppingyvv@me.com**.

_____

_____

_____

_____

Check here: __ Yes, please share my idea.   __ Yes, you can use my name.

                 __ Yes, please email me the free quarterly "tips and ideas" newsletter

Name: _____

Email: _____